MORAL IMAGINATION AND MANAGEMENT DECISION-MAKING

THE RUFFIN SERIES IN BUSINESS ETHICS
R. Edward Freeman, Editor

Moral Imagination and Management Decision-Making

PATRICIA H. WERHANE

New York   Oxford
Oxford University Press
1999

Oxford University Press

Oxford   New York
Athens   Auckland   Bangkok   Bogotá   Buenos Aires   Calcutta
Cape Town   Chennai   Dar es Salaam   Delhi   Florence   Hong Kong   Istanbul
Karachi   Kuala Lumpur   Madrid   Melbourne   Mexico City   Mumbai
Nairobi   Paris   São Paulo   Singapore   Taipei   Tokyo   Toronto   Warsaw

and associated companies in
Berlin   Ibadan

Copyright © 1999 by Oxford University Press, Inc.

Published by Oxford University Press, Inc.,
198 Madison Avenue, New York, New York 10016

Oxford is a registered trademark of Oxford University Press

Library of Congress Cataloging-in-Publication Data
Werhane, Patricia Hogue.
    Moral imagination and management decision making /
    Patricia H. Werhane
        p.   cm.
    Includes bibliographical references and index.
    ISBN 0-19-512569-X
    1. Decision-making—Moral and ethical aspects.
    2. Management—Moral and ethical aspects.   I. Title.
    HD30.23.W467   1998
    658.4′8—dc21   98-17928

9 8 7 6 5 4 3 2 1

Printed in the United States of America
on acid-free paper

For Anna, Kristen, and Nichole

FOREWORD

R. Edward Freeman

It is all too easy to see business ethics as making impossible demands on business people. Especially in a litigious society that often punishes well-meaning decisions after the fact, executives are understandably timid in going out on "ethical limbs" to take a stand about controversial matters. "Ethics versus profits," "stockholders versus stakeholders," "short term versus long term" are just a few of the paradoxes that typically arise in discussions of business ethics.

Patricia Werhane in this marvelous book has suggested that what is lacking in most conversations about the role of ethics in business is the use of imagination. She goes on to develop the concept of "moral imagination" as a way to enrich our understanding of how to manage in a world that is filled with moral challenges. Werhane takes several recent examples from the business world and shows how imagination has been lacking and suggests that there were in fact better decisions to be made. However, executives had to free their imaginations from some traditional mind-sets.

There is a premium in organizations today on "learning" and "knowledge." Business people have understood that the only competitive advantage that is sustainable is the knowledge and skills of their employees, from CEO to security guard. Werhane offers a welcome addition to this literature on organizational learning. Only by recognizing the mind-sets that we use and their limitations can we use our substantial imaginations to improve what we do.

The purpose of the Ruffin Series in Business Ethics is to publish the best thinking about the role of ethics in business. In a world in which there are daily reports of questionable business practices, from financial scandals to environmental disasters, we need to step back from the fray and understand the large issues of how business and ethics are and ought to be connected. The books in this series are aimed at three audiences: management scholars, ethicists, and business executives. There is a growing consensus among these groups that business and ethics must be integrated as a vital part of the teaching and practice of management.

Patricia Werhane has given us a book that will open up new and fertile territory for its readers. She demonstrates through the arguments in this book that there is no more important task for business people than to use their imaginations to create pathways out of traditional ethical dilemmas.

PREFACE

Some time ago David Messick asked me to serve as a commentator at a Northwestern University conference of leading social psychologists on the topic of business ethics. The presenters at this conference, each of whom was well known in social psychology, dealt with ethical issues in business from perspectives with which I was only vaguely familiar. Listening to these papers challenged many of my ingrained assumptions about the application of ethical theory to business. I was forced to rethink seemingly obvious conclusions concerning why ordinary, decent, intelligent managers engage in questionable activities and why, sometimes, these activities are encouraged or even instigated by the climate or culture of companies they manage. I began to realize that ignorance of ethical theory and lack of moral reasoning skills, alone, were not enough to explain this set of phenomena. Nor were widely touted explanations in terms of managerial roles, organizational climate, and role morality sufficient. Something else was involved: a paucity of what I have come to label "moral imagination."

The project was further inspired by Mark Johnson's *Moral Imagination*, a book that helped to focus my thinking about imagination in an applied context. This book is an outcome of those ruminations, and I am gratefully indebted to Mark Johnson for his insights.

Subsequently, I introduced the idea of moral imagination in a more systematic way at the 1994 Ruffin Lectures on New Approaches to Business Ethics sponsored by the Olsson Center for Applied Ethics at the University of Virginia. In responding to my paper, Greg Dees and Kirk Hart helped to clarify the idea of moral imagination. Joanne Ciulla and Deborah Vidaver-Cohen wrote complementary and challenging response papers.

A number of people have been extraordinarily supportive of this project. John Dienhart and Ed Freeman read every chapter and critiqued almost every idea. Jane Collier, John Darley, Alan Singer, Bob Solomon, and an anonymous reviewer for Oxford University Press have provided additional ideas and criticisms, and Norman Bowie and Ronald Duska have straightened out a number of points. Marty Calkins, Robert Phillips, Tara Radin, and Joel Reichart have all listened patiently to more about moral imagination that any one person should be subjected to. Joe Pirri meticulously helped to craft my writing into readable prose. But I am responsible for transforming these ideas, suggestions, and critiques into the book that is the result.

I thank the Olsson Center for Applied Ethics, the Ruffin Foundation, and the Darden Graduate School of Business Administration and Foundation at the University of Virginia for their continued philosophical, economic, and moral support for this project, Henry Tulloch, for editorial assistance, and Susan Lacefield and Karen Musselman for their invaluable secretarial assistance.

ACKNOWLEDGMENTS

Thinking about moral imagination in the context of management decision-making was initiated in my paper "Business Ethics of Risk, Reasoning, and Decision Making" at the Northwestern Conference on Social Psychology and Business Ethics in 1994 and subsequently published in *Codes of Conduct: Behavioral Research into Business Ethics,* ed. David Messick and Ann Tenbrunsel (New York: Russell Sage, 1996).

Selections from chapter 2 appear in an article, "Self-Interests, Roles, and Some Limits to Role Morality," *Public Affairs Quarterly,* 12: 1998. An early version of portions of chapter 3 was published in an article, "Engineers and Management: The Challenge of the Challenger Incident," in the *Journal of Business Ethics,* volume 10, 1991. A shorter version of chapter 4 appears in Laura Pincus Hartman's book *Perspectives on Business Ethics,* published by Sage in 1997. Portions of chapters 5 and 6 appear in *Business Ethics Quarterly: Special Issue: New Approaches to Business Ethics,* 8: 1998. I thank each of these journals for permission to use revised versions of these publications.

The description of the Bronco II test track incidents is quoted from "Legal Maneuvers: Ford Attorneys Played Unusually Large Role in Bronco II's Launch" by Milo Geyelin and Neal Templin in *The Wall Street Journal,* January 5, 1993. Part of the description of the Joseph Jett case was quoted from "Kidder Reports Fraud and Ousts a Top Trader" by Saul Hansell, *The New York Times,* April 18, 1994. Both of these lengthy quotations are reprinted by permission of these newspapers.

CONTENTS

MORAL IMAGINATION AND MANAGEMENT DECISION-MAKING

1

Introduction

Founded in 1906, the family-owned company Malden Mills is one of the last textile mills located in Lawrence, Massachusetts. Most of the US textile industry, formerly located in the northeast of the country, has moved to the South or to Asia, where nonunionized workers and cheaper wages keep these mills competitive. However, Malden Mills, under the direction of Aaron Feuerstein, chose to stay in Lawrence, where his family had always operated this business, and the mill continued to be a unionized workplace.

During the early 1980s, Malden Mills had to lay off workers and was almost bankrupt because of fierce competition in the traditional fabric business. Feuerstein still did not close the plant. Instead, he turned to the union, to his engineers, and to his managers and asked them for ways to help the company become more efficient. Given that challenge, Malden's engineers created a new fabric, Polartec, a patented thermal polyester fleece fabric. This fabric became an almost instant success in the winter clothing market. In the meantime, with the cooperation of the union, Malden's employees were able to reduce the labor component of all fabric production to under 10% of costs. As a result, by 1995, with reduced labor costs and the expanding demand for Polartec, Malden Mills had increased its small labor force to 2,900 people in Lawrence and 3,200 people worldwide. Its sales rose to $400 million and it became highly profitable (Narva, 1996).

Then, on December 11, 1995, the aging Lawrence factory partially burned, putting most of its workers out of jobs. Feuerstein faced a new dilemma. The insurance company would pay only about half of the $300

3

million needed for rebuilding the factory. Feuerstein, at age 70, had to decide whether to go into debt to rebuild the factory.

Feuerstein decided to rebuild Malden Mills as quickly as possible. In the meantime, he continued to pay wages and benefits to his out-of-work employees. Within three months of the fire, the company was again producing Polartec, and most of the workers have jobs at the new plant.

"There was a big history of paternalism, it wasn't just the fire," said Paul Correy, president of the local union, a branch of the Union of Neeedletrades Industry and Textile Employees. "It brought the best out of you. He [Feuerstein] gave you security and you gave him a good day's work" (Goozner, 1996, 27).

> 1993: General Electric's [GE] NBC News unit issues an on-air apology to General Motors [GM] for staging a misleading simulated crash test of GM's full-sized pickup. The model pickup in question was one manufactured between 1973 and 1987 whose alleged problem is its side-saddle gas tank which, like Ford's Pinto, often explodes upon impact. Unfortunately NBC News failed to create an explosion with its simulations, so it planted an explosive inside the pictured pickup gas tank. NBC has agreed to pay GM's estimated $1 million legal and investigation expenses. (Paré, 1994, 46)
> GM alleges that there is nothing wrong with this model pickup, but currently there are over 200 law suits pending against the company for accidents allegedly caused by this model pickup's gas tank. (McCarthy and Lavin, 1993, A2)

> January 1994: A study by the Project on Government Oversight, a Washington watch-dog group, found that General Electric had been involved in more instances of Pentagon fraud since 1990 than any other military contractor. Although it was the fifth-largest military contractor during that period, General Electric had 16 criminal convictions and civil judgments, compared with 4 for McDonnell Douglas, the nation's largest military contractor. (Frantz and Nasar, 1994, A1, C3)

> February 1994: The Justice Department brought a criminal antitrust case against General Electric, accusing it of conspiring with an arm of the South African DeBeers diamond cartel to fix prices in the $600 million world market for industrial diamonds. (Frantz and Nasar, 1994, A1, C3)

> April 18, 1994: Kidder, Peabody & Company [then owned by GE] . . . dismissed its chief government bond trader [Joseph Jett] during the weekend after it had uncovered fraudulent trading apparently

intended to inflate the brokerage firm's profits and the trader's 1993 bonus. As a result, Kidder said $350 million in profits it recorded in the last year never existed. . . . Jett, a 36-year-old managing director . . . was among Kidder's most highly paid employees, earning a bonus of more that $9 million for 1993, the firm said. (Hansell, 1994, A1; see also Paré, 1994, 40–7)[1]

July 19, 1994: The *New York Times* reported that Ian Johnson, an engineer at GE, informed the FBI that GE's jet engines were not meeting safety specifications on either its commercial or its military aircraft engines. The FBI is conducting a lengthy investigation. (Frantz and Nasar, 1994, A1, C3)

Malden Mills and GE are both successful companies managed by chief executive officers (CEOs) often cited for their management and leadership skills. Yet the differences between these two companies, are not merely size, profitability, ownership structure, or diversity. What these differences are and why they matter are the topics for this book.

This book explores the role of moral imagination in managerial and corporate decision-making. My aim is to develop some fresh insights on two simple questions: Why do ordinary, decent managers engage in questionable behavior? Why do successful companies ignore the ethical dimensions of their processes, decisions, and actions? In what follows, I argue that the missing element in many instances of alleged managerial or corporate wrongdoing is a simple phenomenon: moral imagination.

Moral imagination refers to the ability to perceive that a web of competing economic relationships is, at the same time, a web of moral relationships. Developing moral imagination means becoming sensitive to ethical issues in business decision making, but it also means searching out places where people are likely to be hurt by decision making or behavior of managers. This moral imagination is a necessary first step, but because of prevailing methods of evaluating managers on bottom-line results, it is extremely challenging. It is essential, however, before anything else can happen. (Carroll, 1987, 13, reprinted with some modifications from Powers and Vogel, 1980, 40)

By "moral imagination" I include the awareness of various dimensions of a particular context as well as its operative framework and narratives. Moral imagination entails the ability to understand that context or set of activities from a number of different perspectives, the actualizing of new possibilities that are not context-dependent, and the instigation of the process of evaluating those possibilities from a moral point of view. It is the latter that distinguishes *moral* imagination. Joseph Jett was imaginative, but behaved in a morally questionable manner. Jack Welch, the CEO of GE, is enormously creative, but GE does not always judge its creative ventures from the point of view of independent moral standards. Thus,

I shall argue, moral imagination is a necessary ingredient in management decision-making. Otherwise, one often gets trapped in a particular "schema" or narrative that fails to take into account important dimensions of one's activities. This entrapment may lead to difficulties or even disasters. What distinguishes Aaron Feuerstein and Malden Mills is that, when financially challenged, he and his managers were enormously imaginative in creating a financially successful solution. At the same time, Feuerstein perceived that "the web of competing economic relationships" at Malden Mills was "a web of moral relationships." He could not disengage his business decisions from the moral standards he set for himself and for Malden Mills. Feuerstein's success is, in great measure, due to his ability to integrate these standards in his quest for new products and fiscal solvency. This, indeed, takes moral imagination.

If ethics simply involved evaluating questionable people or questionable institutions engaged in bad behavior, there would be many fewer ethical *issues*. In the 1960s an insurance company, Equity Funding, short of customers, made up clients, issued bogus policies to these nonexistent persons, and then resold those policies to an insurance holding company. This scheme, which went on undetected for several years, was clearly unethical and illegal as well. The only issue in that case was whether the whistleblower, James Dirks, did something unethical or illegal by selling his clients' stock in Equity Funding before reporting the scheme to the Securities Exchange Commission (SEC) (Dirks and Gross, 1974; Sturdivant, 1977, 17–31).

However, most ethical issues in business are not a result of clear-cut misbehavior. They usually involve smart managers and reputable companies that somehow, like GE, create scenarios that have untoward consequences. Let us look at some other examples. Union Carbide was and is a very fine company. Its former CEO, Warren Anderson, was a self-effacing, deeply religious person of the highest moral character. Before 1984 Union Carbide's safety record, with all their chemical plants worldwide, was exemplary. Yet despite its expertise in safety, the company built a plant in Bhopal, India, that was to defy many of Union Carbide's own safety standards and eventually leak a deadly chemical that killed over 2,500 people (Shrivastava, 1987).

The Swiss-based Nestlé Company produces some of the finest quality infant formula and is well known as expert in international marketing. Beginning in the 1950s, Nestlé took well-tested marketing strategies for infant formula to developing countries in Africa, plans that had been successful in Europe, North America, and parts of Asia. Although Nestlé was expert at manufacturing quality products and in predicting customer needs, as a result of its marketing strategies in East Africa, maternal misuse of the formula cost the lives of thousands of babies fed formula instead of being nursed (Sethi, 1994).

The *Challenger* space shuttle was a joint project of NASA and a number of excellent subcontractors including Morton Thiokol, a corporation created by a merger of two highly reputable companies. Before the 1986 *Challenger* explosion there had been only one accident during the history of NASA's space flights, and 24 previous launches of space shuttles constructed almost identically to the *Challenger* had proceeded without problems. Despite NASA's fine safety record and Thiokol's expertise in space travel, on the 25th mission of the space shuttle program on January 28, 1986, the *Challenger* exploded within 60 seconds of liftoff (Werhane, 1991b, 605–7).

Why do these tragic events occur? The former Federal Reserve chairperson, Paul Volcker, argues that the common thread in these scenarios is "good, old-fashioned greed" (quoted in Bacon and Salwen, 1991, A10). But that explanation, while probably partially true, is not altogether satisfactory. Except for Kidder's chief bond trader Joseph Jett, the participants in these activities were hardly in need of money, and in fact GE and its subsidiaries have suffered financially as a result of these incidents. In the NBC–GE/GM case, NBC has paid GM over a million dollars in damages. And GM is still embroiled in civil suits concerning the full-sized pickup. Jett, specifically, lost a great deal by being caught. Because he banked his bonus at Kidder, Kidder kept the $9 million it had paid him in 1993.

This set of cases raises some simple questions. How do some good managers or companies maintain consistency in their standards of behavior? Why do others engage in questionable behavior? How is it that ordinary actions of many well-intentioned managers and reputable companies are exemplary; how is that similar actions by others produce terrible consequences? Ethical issues in business, like those in personal life, are troublesome, the more so because most managers in today's open and competitive economy are smart, well-intentioned people, and the companies they manage ordinarily intentionally try to avoid egregious behavior. Why is it, then, that some become involved in questionable activities or produce harm while others do not? Is merely human fallibility the cause, or is something more at stake?

A second set of questions derives from the GE cases. Most managers and most companies are not without ethical difficulties. Indeed, it would be strange if they were, because neither people nor the companies they constitute are infallible. But the problem is not merely a one-time weakness of will, but what I would call moral amnesia, an inability to remember or learn from one's own and others' past mistakes and to transfer that knowledge when fresh challenges arise. The Joseph Jett scandal was closely preceded by a similar problem at Salomon Brothers two years earlier when its head of Treasury bond trading, Paul Mozer, was caught buying bonds in his customers' accounts without their knowledge. As a result, in three fiscal quarters Mozer purchased more Treasury Bonds for Salomon than was legally allowed, giving Salomon control of the Treasury bond market for these three quarters (Bacon and Salwen, 1991, A10; Bartlett, 1991, 1). The Salomon Brothers events were front-page headlines for months, and its three top managers as well as Mozer were fired. Did Jett not relate those incidents to his own situation?

The Ford Pinto explosions in the 1970s are a set of cases well documented at Ford, in the courts, and by the media. Having witnessed the problems of Ford's Pinto, GM nevertheless refused to recall its full-size pickups manufactured between 1973 and 1987, pickups whose fuel tank placement presents risks similar to those experienced by Pinto owners. More recently, Ford engineers developed, tested, and eventually manufactured a utility vehicle, the Bronco II. During tests for the prototype of this car in 1982, it was discovered that the front wheel of the vehicle tended to lift off on the test track curve at speeds over 40 miles an hour. Although the tests were witnessed by Ford's legal counsel and the company's head of safety, according to reports in the *Wall Street Journal*, Ford went ahead with the manufacture of the Bronco II without design changes, this time carefully shredding the documents describing the test failures(Geyelin and Templin, 1993, A1, 6).[2]

These cases, and others, tell a story about business, and it is not a positive story. Most of the cases I have cited in this chapter create the impression that business is bad and that free enterprise political economies are in moral trouble. But that is not true. There are thousands of managers like Aaron Feuerstein and hundreds of companies like Malden Mills engaged in the practice of commerce in a morally exemplary manner. This is why other cases are troublesome. None of these incidents need to have occurred, nor should they have been repeated. They create a false impression that business is not a morally worthwhile enterprise, although, as I argue, this is not true. But in order to tell a positive story about business, we have to figure out how to avoid these needless negative outcomes.

There is a third set of issues I investigate in this book:

> In 1986, CBS's program *60 Minutes* alleged that the automatic transmissions of the 1978–1986 models of the Audi 5000 German automobile had an accelerator defect. In at least 750 cases drivers who claimed to have put their foot on the brake said that the car accelerated. A number of deaths were attributed to this phenomenon. As a result, Audi lost over 80% of its US market share in automobile sales. (Yates, 1986, W31).

> It turned out, after extensive investigation, that in each of those cases the driver had put his or her foot on the accelerator! (Zverina, 1989, F1,5)

These cases illustrate how a certain set of beliefs or a narrative becomes so dominant that we begin to believe that narrative without verifying its truth. We organize our experience through a nexus of mental models that create a series of stories or narratives. When one narrative becomes widely accepted, it can affect one's judgment and bias the ways one deals with other facts even to the extent of excluding from consideration or even falsifying verifiable data. Potential Audi buyers simply believed the *60 Minutes* report to such an extent that even when the facts of the cases were uncovered and again revealed on a later *60 Minutes* program, Audi's market share suffered for several years afterward.

The role of narratives is important in some of the other cases I have cited as well. It is reported that Paul Mozer, the Treasury bond trader at Salomon, thought he was playing a game with the Treasury Department in which the aim was to outwit it. He thus may have created a narrative, an interpretation of reality that Treasury bond trading was a game like chess, and one explanation of his behavior is that Mozer bought into that narrative despite its fantasy (Bartlett, 1991, C1; Murray, 1991, A1). Similarly, according to at least two commentators, after numerous successful launches NASA officials began to think that the agency was invincible and that the space shuttle was a perfect, even risk-free vehicle (Feynman, 1989, 179–83; Schwartz, 1987, 56–67). The consequences of accepting these narratives in both cases is obvious.

This book begins with an exploration of a number of tempting ways to approach these complex issues of intentionality and moral accountability. If "good, old-fashioned greed" is a factor, we need to investigate the role of self-interest in managerial decision-making. It will turn out, however, that self-interests are complex matters, that people are motivated by other interests including genuine interests in other people, and that egoism, alone, is a defective mechanism for explaining the complex cases I have cited.

According to the moral development literature, a second option is to speculate that managers at Ford and Nestlé, Union Carbide and Thiokol, Jett, and perhaps even the top management at Kidder operated on the lowest level of moral development, gauging their moral judgments on what Lawrence Kohlberg and other psychologists call the preconventional level, using self-interest and personal gain as the only goal of their activities, and basing their actions simply on whether they would be caught. This analysis might be plausible to describe Jett, although there is independent evidence of his strong moral upbringing, but it hardly describes most managerial decision-making. It is true that most managers act for the self-interest of their companies, and one can safely conclude that no one wants to get caught engaged in wrongdoing. Yet evidence from a number of studies suggests that most managers operate at least on the conventional moral development level; they care a great deal about interrelationships and appeal to conventions, social mores, and the law to guide their actions (Derry, 1989). Mozer and Jett may have been caught up in their own self-interest, but it appeared to be primarily in the form of an interest to win and to show their employers that they were good at trading.

Alternately, one could conclude that managers of companies in trouble are of weak moral character, that they do not exhibit the virtues of excellence, honor, and respect for community (Solomon, 1992). This, too, is a difficult contention to verify, and again, there is contrary evidence that people like Warren Anderson, the engineers at Thiokol and at NASA, and Nestlé's top management are basically decent, even personally virtuous people.

There is still another set of explanations of moral amnesia. Each of us, as a member of a particular society embedded in family, religious, social, political relationships and as a professional, a manager, or an employee, has, or acquires, a number of social roles. These roles are defined by the social institutions in which one finds oneself or is a member. Sometimes these roles and their concomitant responsibilities overwhelmingly shape one's worldview and strongly influence one's judgments. We find, for example, religious zealots so committed to a cause or, on a smaller scale, employees so committed to their company and its survival that they will perform activities unconscionable or even absurd to the ordinary outsider. The numerous managers at Equity Funding who participated in the activities of making up clients, creating their personal history and medical records, and who wrote policies on behalf of these mythical customers exemplify role commitment that clearly went amok. Their perceived commitment to keep Equity Funding in business overrode ordinary role expectations for a good insurance company manager, as well as customary moral considerations and legal requirements. That this behavior might be a conflict of interest did not deter Equity Funding managers from continuing their fraudulent practices. The Equity Funding case, fortunately, is an exception to management practice, but it illustrates a recurring organizational phenomenon.

Moral philosophers offer another set of reasons. Few managers have had serious training in moral philosophy, nor do many of them understand the nuances of deontology, utilitarianism, rights theory, and theories of virtue or justice. There is a set of arguments that develops the thesis that training in moral reasoning might increase moral awareness, facilitate moral decision-making, and, it is proposed, prevent may of the problems from occurring. Moral education, if complete, would prevent many of the incidents I have cited, according to this thesis. It will turn out, however, that the simple teaching and application of moral principles or rules may not alleviate all problems. It is not always lack of logic or ignorance of moral principles that causes these problems but the principles' general character that fails in specificity of application. This specificity has not so much to do with the particular situation at issue, per se, but rather with how the situation is perceived and framed by its protagonists. For example, during the Pinto era at Ford, according to many of its managers who were there at that time, almost no one at Ford raised an issue about the manufacture and sale of the Pinto, even when burned-out Pintos were returned to the factory (Gioia, 1991, 382–5). Similarly, according to insiders, Paul Mozer, the bond trader at Salomon, seemed, at least outwardly, to bracket moral considerations, even the question of breaking the law or being found out, except as those considerations related to the game of trading. Even after being condemned by the World Health Organization (WHO) for its marketing practices in Africa, Nestlé failed to change these procedures for some years, claiming innocence of any wrongdoing. Moreover, Ford, GE, and other companies have codes of ethics, and GE has an extensive ethics program for its managers. What is evident, then, in these cases is not weak moral development, a failure of moral character, or lack of understanding what is right or wrong, but rather a setting aside of moral considerations in the pace of business activities. So simply learning about moral reasoning or moral theory, in the abstract, by itself, does not appear to be enough unless one somehow integrates those reasoning skills in actual practice.

In this book I shall argue that most individual managers are not without moral sensibilities or values, nor are they motivated merely by greed or even self-interest, nor are most of these managers at a low level of moral development. Companies, too, are not without moral sensibilities, and many corporations such as GE have a values statement and an ethics program for managers. Nevertheless, in many situations managers have a narrow perspective on their situation and little in the way of moral imagination. As Paul Mozer and Joseph Jett illustrate, some managers confuse reality with what they want it to be. Others lack a sense of the variety of possibilities and moral consequences of their decisions, as well as the ability to imagine a wide range of possible issues, consequences, and solutions. Some individuals and institutions are trapped in the framework of history, organization, corporate culture, and tradition of which they are only at best vaguely aware, a framework that often drives their decision-making to preclude taking into account moral concerns, a framework that sometimes even allows or encourages managers to overestimate their powers and abilities. Still other managers are so focused on their roles and role responsibilities to a particular organization that they fail to consider simple norms of morality.

To account for these phenomena, I shall make a very simple point. All reality is socially structured. All experience is interpreted or constituted by a conceptual scheme and an overlapping set of incomplete mental models through which we selectively frame, order, organize, and interpret the data of experience. Each of us functions through a set of mental models that are socially learned, culturally inculcated, educationally reinforced, and experientially altered. These mental models are necessarily incomplete and volatile; that is, they can be relearned and changed. They are neither universally, socially, institutionally, nor culturally the same in every individual, although they overlap and are socially, institutionally, and culturally shared or shareable with others. In some settings certain mental models function as scripts that focus our attention on a particular set of habits for dealing with that set of events in that context. In those cases these mental models serve as focusing mechanisms to bracket out other points of view or other schema. Thus, I shall argue, the kinds of mental models operative in any setting create decision-making habits that may preclude taking into account some important data. For example, as I shall argue in more detail, the fact that NASA had a long string of successes may have created a mental model of optimism that could have precluded some of its engineers from taking initially overcautious safety measures before each launch. Nestlé's belief that infant formula, in many cases, is superior to breast milk and its successes in a number of international markets framed its managerial decision-making and marketing practices so that perhaps its executives did not understand what was at issue in the company's African markets.

Moreover, all human experiences are embedded in a set of narratives, many of which are not of one's own making. We are born into a particular historical tradition, and we find ourselves part of religious, social, and cultural traditions embedded in a language. We do not choose these traditions and narratives, nor can we always escape them. Sometimes these narratives can be distorting, as the Audi and breast implant cases illustrate. Still, I shall argue further, none of us is merely defined by our background narratives. Each of us is an author of, as well as a participant in, our own history and narratives.

Therefore, even though all experience is interpreted, reality is socially constituted, and our experiences are embedded in series of narratives, I shall argue that who we are, what we do, and how we behave are not merely narrative-driven or conceptually constrained. There are at least two reasons why this is so. First, I shall argue, the self cannot be merely equated with its roles and social relationships, despite the impossibility of getting at the self apart from those roles and relationships. Thus, the existence of some narrow-minded decision-making, or the dominance of strongly differentiated role responsibilities, does not morally excuse misbehavior or the occurrence of untoward consequences that could have been avoided. Second, because mental models and narratives are incomplete and overlap, human choices are not merely context-determined. Underlying all human activity is what Donald Davidson calls a "common coordinate system" (Davidson, 1974, 5) that accounts for human understanding and communication and for the fact that any particular mental model can be examined and revised.

One of the primary reasons for the undesirable outcomes in the cases I have cited is a paucity of moral imagination. Most managers and their institutions do not lack moral principles. Rather, they sometimes have a narrow perspective on their situation. They lack a sense of the variety of possibilities and moral consequences of their decisions and the ability to imagine a wide range of issues, consequences, and solutions. Some individuals are trapped in an organizational framework and tradition of which they are only vaguely aware, a framework that often drives their decision-making and excludes considerations of moral concerns. Managers do not always remember and thus learn from their mistakes, because they do not realize they have made mistakes. Sometimes, too, a dominant narrative creates a story that, while plausible, distorts and narrows the frame of decision-making.

A developed moral imagination gives managers means to disengage themselves from a particular situation, from its narrative, from one's roles, and from a dominating conceptual scheme. Moral imagination enables one to assess one's situation, to evaluate present and new possibilities, and to create decisions that are not parochially embedded in a restricted context or confined by a certain point of view. Without moral imagination, mistakes are reiterated.

However, one should not confuse moral imagination with practical moral reasoning. The book concludes with the thesis that moral imagination is a necessary but not a sufficient condition for creative moral managerial decision-making. Without moral imagination one can easily be drawn into a particular mindset that does not take into account other critical perspectives. On the other hand, imagination alone can create fantasies that, too, become dominating and falsifying narratives, as the Audi case illustrates. I shall therefore argue that moral reasoning is a crucial element in management decision-making, an element that nevertheless depends on moral imagination as its driving force and on moral standards as its "bottom line." Practical moral reasoning takes into account ethical theory but not abstractly. Moral reasoning begins with the particular—a specific scenario. This is because in the first instance ethics has to do with human relationships and human activities, not with abstract formal principles. It generates conclusions from that particular set of events, taking into account not merely the situation but its narrative and the set of mental models or conceptual schemes that frames these events. Moral imagination is essential to get one from a particular situation to a more disengaged perspective. At the same time, moral reasoning helps to challenge any event with stipulative principles or minimum moral standards that are not context-dependent or merely forms of role morality. Management decision-making, then, must be contextual, imaginative, and rational. It must begin with the particular, but go beyond that, in order to avoid obvious errors of judgment.

Moral imagination and moral reasoning provide concrete managerial decision-making skills with which to avoid questionable activities, prevent unseemly consequences, and enable a manager or a company to create decision models that contribute positively to corporate and societal well-being. I shall conclude by citing a number of cases in which imaginative decision-making has enabled or even driven managers to be creative, profitable, and morally exemplary. Companies such as Levi Strauss, Johnson & Johnson, Merck, South Shore Bank, and others have, in certain circumstances, gone beyond what is expected in the processes of ordinary managerial decision-making. These managers and their companies knowingly and creatively exhibit moral imagination, an imagination "disciplined by respect for the real" (Tuan, 1989, 10). They take moral risks, and they exhibit exemplary moral leadership while continuing to be profitable. With their moral imaginations fully at work, they become, in Henry James's words, "finely aware and richly responsible" (James, 1934, 62, cited in Nussbaum, 1990, 111).

2

Some Partial Solutions

Joseph Jett, the dismissed bond trader at Kidder Peabody, a division of GE at the time of the incident, is an African-American and a graduate of MIT. He attended the Harvard Business School but did not complete a degree. Before being hired by Kidder in 1991, Jett had been a so-so bond trader at First Boston and then at Morgan Stanley. Jett soon become one of Kidder's best producers and was promoted to managing director and head of the government trading desk, supervising 16 other traders. All went well for Jett, and because of his successful management and trading, in 1992 he was awarded a $9 million bonus.

Jett reported to Edward Cerullo, known for his "hands-off" management style. According to a number of reports, previous to the Jett incident, Kidder had had some difficulties with other traders. Linda LaPrade, a former Kidder trader, alleged that Cerullo "pressured her to inflate bids for government 'agency' securities . . . and threaten[ed] her with termination if she didn't comply" (Cohen, Freedman, and Power, 1994, A1). In 1991 Kidder and Cerullo were fined because of the activities of a Kidder trader, Ira Saferstein, "which [allegedly] involved Mr. Saferstein's profiting from a customer error" (Cohen, Freedman, and Power, 1994, A8). According to at least one report, in 1992 Hugh Bush, who worked with Jett, accused Jett of "'mismarking,' or misrecording, trading positions, which is illegal" (Cohen, Freedman, and Power, 1994, A8). Other traders claim Bush was then fired because of these accusations. Cerullo denied that charge. According to *Fortune*, at least one trader at Kidder, Charles Sheehan, was not licensed to be a broker; neither was the head of Kidder, Michael Carpenter (Paré, 1994, 42).

15

On April 18, 1994, Kidder announced the dismissal of Jett for fraudulent trading. According to reports, Jett apparently covered up losses and
inflated profits by conducting a series of phantom trades of government
bonds (Alexander, 1994, B1; Siconolfi, 1994, A1, A4).

The New York Times reported:

> Kidder said [Jett's] plan involved a phony series of large trades to recon-
> stitute zero-coupon bonds into regular bonds, known as "recon" trades. It
> was said to have taken advantage of the differences between how regular
> bonds and zero-coupon bonds are traded and entered on a firm's books.
>
> Regular bonds are quoted in terms of the face value of the bond. It is
> understood that when a trade is consummated, the seller will also pay the
> buyer an amount equal to the interest that has been earned on the bond
> but that has not been paid by the Government. With zero-coupon bonds,
> the interest earned is factored into the quoted price. Even if the bond
> market does not move, the price of a zero-coupon bond will rise every day
> to account for the earned interest.
>
> Mr. Jett entered a series of "forward recon" trades into Kidder's books,
> according to John Liftin, the firm's general counsel. These trades indi-
> cated an intention to reconstitute zero-coupon bonds at some point in the
> future. While many other bond market transactions are traded to be com-
> pleted in the future, known as forward trades, there are no such forward
> trades for recons, Mr. Liftin said. Still, Kidder's computer system accepted
> the transactions.
>
> A forward recon trade appeared to Kidder's computer to create a profit
> because of the differences in the way interest is calculated. . . . The dif-
> ference would in theory have disappeared on the day in the future that
> the trade was scheduled to be consummated, but Mr. Jett kept postponing
> the trades, increasing their size. (Hansell, 1994, A1)

Jett was immediately dismissed from Kidder, and because he had de-
posited his bonus in a Kidder account, it was confiscated by that company. And GE, the parent of Kidder, took a $350 million loss for that fis-
cal quarter.

Jett claims he was set up as a "scapegoat to deflect scrutiny of [Kid-
der's] mortgage-bond woes" (Siconolfi, 1994, A4). The *New York Post* and
Black Enterprise support that contention, saying that Jett was "set up as
the distraction for Kidder's losses, as well as its systemic lack of supervi-
sory controls" (Mack, 1994, 28).

Since the time of Aristotle, people have been debating why good people
engage in questionable moral behavior and even repeat their mistakes.
General Electric is commonly cited as one of the best companies in
America (e.g., Bollier, 1996; Collins and Porras, 1994). Consistently
profitable, the company is constantly evolving to meet changing global
demands, and books have been written about the successful management style of its current CEO, Jack Welch (e.g., Tichy and Sherman,
1993). At the same time GE has not avoided ethical difficulties, some of
which I cited in the last chapter. The Joseph Jett incident is merely one

illustration. Why do these incidents continue to occur in a company as fine as GE? Why do they sometimes reoccur? In this chapter I explore a number of explanations for these phenomena.

It is often argued that human beings are motivated primarily by self-interest; in business, managerial or corporate self-interest, sometimes even greed, accounts for questionable and even egregious behavior. Moreover, none of us is perfect, so in large companies such as GE there are bound to be errors of judgment. From the psychology of moral development literature, one might conclude that some of these people have a low level of moral development; hence, they act without much regard either for the social or legal networks of relationships or for the consequences of their actions to themselves, to other people, or to their company.

Other explanations also attempt to account for these events and their perpetrators. Each of the cases cited in chapter 1 occurs in a sociocultural and legal framework. It is then sometimes argued that social, political, and legal institutions, along with the corporate culture and the particular roles and role responsibilities of the managers and companies in question, create a causal nexus that constrains what we as outsiders might consider morally appropriate behavior and often precludes the consequential avoidance of harm.

Finally, both on the individual and corporate level, it is sometimes argued that many companies and their managers either are unaware of the moral dimensions of their activities or lack skills in moral reasoning. According to this argument, proper moral education could raise the level of individual and institutional moral awareness, enhance moral development, and give managers theoretical tools from moral theory with which to deal with ethical issues. These managers, then, fully trained in moral reasoning and moral theory, would apply such training to their decision processes with more positive results.

In what follows I examine all of these explanations and approaches. Each of them, it will turn out, focuses on a part of what is important in managerial and corporate moral decision-making; each will aid my analysis of these questions throughout the book. However, none of the approaches I outline in what follows exhaustively answers my questions: Why do ordinarily decent managers or reputable companies get into trouble? Why do they sometimes repeat their mistakes? None of these explanations deals with the role of moral imagination in ethical decision-making.

HUMAN NATURE AND SELF-INTEREST

All companies consist of people, and people are seldom morally perfect by almost any measure of morality. It follows that companies, like individuals, will likely make moral mistakes. This seems obvious, and it is also obvious that most of us repeat our mistakes at least some of the time. But it is not obvious why managers, faced with issues similar to those they have faced in the past, when those former issues were public incidents that received media, regulatory, and public attention, repeat similar mistakes. The Joseph Jett incident followed a series of morally questionable activities at GE; it also followed closely the very public scandal at Salomon Brothers, where its chief government bond trader, Paul Mozer, and Salomon's three top corporate officers were dismissed after Mozer was caught manipulating Salomon's share of government Treasury bonds.

If Paul Volcker is correct that a motive is "good, old-fashioned greed," one would conclude that Jett and other managers simply acted in their own self-interest, trying to accumulate as much wealth for themselves as possible by manipulating the system. Volcker's assessment is surely partly accurate. But what do we mean when we say that Jett acted in his own self-interest or GE's aberrations are all a matter of old-fashioned greed. It may turn out that acting in one's own self-interest is a complex matter indeed.

To think through the role of self-interest as a motivating force, let us turn to the philosophy of Adam Smith. I go back to Smith because he and Thomas Hobbes are both often cited, along with Bernard Mandeville, as the fathers of psychological egoism, the view that human beings "naturally" and primarily act in their own self-interest. At least in the case of Smith, this is simply a misreading. The Nobel Prize economist George Stigler asserts that Smith's well-known work *The Wealth of Nations* "is a stupendous palace erected upon the granite of self-interest" (1971, 265). According to Stigler, Smith argued that business people, acting in their own interest in the marketplace of commerce and trade, will, even unwittingly, create wealth and economic growth for the political economy in which they operate and even create well-being for those who do not participate directly in commerce. This interpretation of Smith's famous *invisible hand* argument is well known and need not be rehearsed again here. However, it may be helpful to trace the roots of Smith's alleged point of view, a view, I have argued elsewhere, that belies what he says in his earlier work, *The Theory of Moral Sentiments* (*TMS*), and is contrary to his full analysis in *The Wealth of Nations* (Werhane, 1991a).

In *TMS* Smith makes some interesting observations about the nature of self-interest. The idea of any state of nature, even a hypothetical one such as Hobbes proposes, where each of us is an isolated independent being, is alien to Smith's description of human nature. Smith says, "[I]t is thus that man, who can subsist only in society, was fitted by nature to that situation for which he was made" (1759/1976, II.ii.3.1). As a social being dependent on and interacting with others, I am the subject of my interests, so there is a trivial sense in which all my interests are "self-interests." That is, they are the interests *of* the self. But I am not always the *object* of those interests. Human beings "by nature" are endowed with at least three kinds of drives, each having different objects directed to the self (the selfish passions), to others (the social passions), or in reaction to others (the unsocial passions). Each of the first two drives or passions has its virtues and vices: the virtue of the selfish passions is prudence, their vice is selfishness; the virtues of the social passions are benevolence and justice; their vices are malevolence and injustice. Thus, according to Smith, each of us is the subject of and motivated by our passions and interests, but many of our passions and interests are other-directed. Acting altruistically or dispassionately is as natural as acting in one's own self-interest or even selfishly. This does not mean that all of us are alike; some of us are more selfish or more generous or have a stronger commitment to fairness than others. But no one of these passions is more "natural" than any other, and the interests of the self are more or less equally directed to the self and to others (Smith, 1759, I and II).

The statement that someone or some company acted in its own self-interest presents a series of complex considerations. One would want to distinguish first what sort of self-interest the individual or company was acting in and then determine whether the individual or the company was both the subject and the object of that self-interest. For example, one will remember the famous Johnson & Johnson (J&J) Tylenol case. In 1982, after a number of poisoning incidents involving Tylenol capsules occurring over several years, the CEO of J&J James Burke, in consultation with his top managers at J&J, withdrew Tylenol capsules from the market and discontinued their manufacture. Burke and other J&J executives made this decision despite the fact that there was no correlation between J&J's capsule manufacture and the poisoning, and despite the fear that by removing the capsules from the market, J&J would lose its dominant market share in pain medication. The withdrawal of the Tylenol capsule was a decision that contradicted the advice of J&J's legal counsel, who was worried that the withdrawal would be an admission of corporate culpability. The FBI, too, counseled Burke not to withdraw the capsules, since the company was not at fault for the poisoning incidents. Nevertheless, citing J&J's credo, the first lines of which state, "We believe our first responsibility is to the doctors, nurses and patients, to mothers and all others who use our products and services" (Smith and Tedlow, 1989), Burke withdrew the capsules from the shelves, declaring that Tylenol capsules would never again be manufactured or sold.

In this case, J&J was the subject of Burke's actions. But the object of his decision was the interests of the customers, even when that decision threatened J&J's own self-reflective interests to be profitable and to continue a well-known and popular line of pain medications. One might argue that Burke's decision was in J&J's long-term self-interest as well; that is true. But one could not have predicted in advance that J&J would be successful in recapturing the pain medication market share it temporarily lost by removing Tylenol capsules from the market. Indeed, most "experts" predicted the opposite consequence.

Second, acting in one's own interest where one's well-being is the object as well as the subject of action does not necessarily exclude taking into account the interests of others, for those interests are almost always necessary to achieve success. Indeed, if Smith is right about the social nature of human beings, it is impossible not to take others into account, if only negatively. So even if one is cynical about J&J's decision in the Tylenol case, even if it was only trying to save the product and the company, the result took into account customers and was good for all stakeholders.

Third, acting in one's own self interests in either sense is not necessarily evil. One must be careful to distinguish not only the quality of the action itself and its object, for example, oneself or one's company, but also the motivation, for example, greed, self-interest, or the well-being of certain stakeholders, and what in fact that action produces. Many self-interested, even greedy actions do not harm others. If, for example, Joseph Jett became a bond trader in order to amass a fortune, he would not be alone in that motivation nor necessarily a bad person. But when self-interest overwhelms propriety, morality, or law, such actions become unconscionable. While one questions Ivan Boesky's famous alleged statement that "greed is good" (Boesky, 1986), one must nevertheless be careful not to equate all self-interest with greed or to proclaim that acting in one's own self-interest is *always* morally questionable. Interestingly, in the Joseph Jett case, Jett and Kidder had only a little to gain, personally or on a corporate level, from Jett's phantom trading, and it turned out not to be in either Jett's or Kidder's long-term self-interest. So analyzing corporate or managerial wrongdoing or unintentional harm from the perspective of self-interest or greed does not always get us very far. Something else is at stake.

THE CASE FOR MORAL DEVELOPMENT

Still, it is tempting to conclude that Jett and perhaps even the top management at Kidder gauged their moral judgments mostly by focusing on their own personal gain as the object of their self-interest and based their actions on whether they would be caught. According to moral psychologists, such as Lawrence Kohlberg, if that were true, Jett and his colleagues at Kidder would be operating at a low level of moral development.

Kohlberg and his followers have argued that in growing up human beings go through stages of moral development, just as they go through stages of cognitive development, and that each stage depends on the preceding one. It has been well documented that we do develop cognitively, grounding more complex learning experiences on simpler ones. Similarly, Kohlberg argued, people go through stages of moral learning. As small children, we focus primarily on ourselves. In what Kohlberg labeled two preconventional stages of development, children focus on rewards and punishments for their own behavior; they are obedient precisely because they are afraid of getting caught and being punished, and they focus on satisfying their own needs, gauging their relationships with others in terms of what others can do for them. According to Kohlberg, in these two early stages each of us is both egocentric and naively consequentialist, seeking primarily to avoid punishment and to achieve personal gains. In his studies of human behavior Kohlberg found, interestingly, that many criminals function primarily at these two low stages of moral development.

If we follow the path of normal development, Kohlberg argued, as teenagers and as adults we reach two conventional stages of development. In the third stage we are highly socialized conformists; we look to peers and other groups for behavioral expectations, approval, or disapproval. At the fourth stage we become law abiding; we follow rules, respect authority, and develop a sense of duty in relation to the law or society (Kohlberg, 1969/1981).

Kohlberg also posited two postconventional stages of moral development wherein we are able to identify and apply more universal moral values or rules. At these stages, as free autonomous selves, we judge both our own behavior and that of social groups, cultures, and communities to which we and others belong. As we develop to these highest stages, we first make moral judgments on the basis of utility and social contracts and then on the basis of universal principles of justice and the equality of human rights (Kohlberg, 1969). Given these postconventional stages, Kohlberg and his students and followers tested people to find out at what stage they operated. Later psychologists, such as James Rest, have devised educational methodologies and forms of moral education that allegedly advance students' level of moral development, and thus, ultimately, they conclude, improve behavior (Rest, 1988, 1994).

Kohlberg's theory of moral development is highly controversial, and the existence and content of moral stages as Kohlberg depicted them have come under scrutiny. One of the best-known critiques was formulated by one of Kohlberg's former students, Carol Gilligan. Gilligan questioned what she initially found to be gender differences between male and female stages of moral development. Although the relationship between gender difference and types of moral development is also controversial, her work has shown that not all of us experience Kohlberg's stages of moral development, particularly the conventional and postconventional stages as he described them. Gilligan and others depict Kohlberg's description of moral development as too formal and abstract. They find that it focuses on the primacy of the individual in all stages of moral development, as distinct from the individual in the context of social relationships, and that it imagines that one could achieve complete autonomy when developing universally acceptable and applicable principles of fairness without consideration of context or particular social situation (Gilligan, 1982; Kohlberg, Levine, and Hewer, 1983).

While agreeing with Kohlberg that the preconventional stages are egoistic ones, Gilligan describes moral development as the development from simple to more complex social relationships, where one becomes attached to others and responsible for oneself and others in these relationships. Gilligan describes the conventional stages as a development of interrelationships and caring for others. At the highest stages of moral development, one has both a strong sense of self and of others in a network of interrelationships that are, at the same time, caring, attached, and interdependent (Gilligan, 1982).

Much can be learned from the work of Kohlberg, Gilligan, and their followers. From their studies one can conclude that people deal with moral issues differently, some of us more naively than others, some of us primarily from self-interest, some of us depending on law, convention, and social relationships, and others seeking more ideal or universal principles through which to ground and evaluate moral decisions. At the same time, Gilligan is surely correct that one cannot extricate oneself from all human social relationships; indeed, that extrication itself would be a social act. Human relationships play central roles in moral decision-making at every level. None of us lives in a human vacuum. We are born into and affected by human relationships, even in acts of solitude and rejection, and these relationships are part of being moral or immoral (Friedman, 1993, 62–88; Smith, 1759). Kohlberg's highest stage of moral development, the postconventional levels, postulate abstract moral principles, standards that are independent of particular situations and social relationships. If, however, we cannot achieve total independence or autonomy that is not in some way connected to, and an outcome of, social relationships, then the status of these abstract principles comes into question. Moreover, it is impossible to verify universal absolute moral principles. Nevertheless, Kohlberg pointed to a human tendency to set out certain principles as ideals or as candidates for universal principles.[1] One could speculate that in the highest stages of moral development people have a good sense of the self in relationship with others; relate to, respect, and even care about each other; and set out stipulative candidates for moral principles as possible evaluative and judgmental ideals. Moreover, whether or not each of us goes through stages of moral development in ways Kohlberg or Gilligan describes, still, part of the ability to be morally imaginative depends on the ability to evaluate moral stances critically and even the reasoning processes of oneself, one's company, and one's community. Jett appeared to have an inability to make such critical evaluations; thus, he had not developed to this stage of critical moral reasoning and moral imagination, at least in his bond trading ventures.[2]

Most advocates of moral development argue that ethics can be taught to adults—that one can improve the moral development, and thus the character and ultimately the behavior, of adults. According to Rest,

> [d]ramatic and extensive changes occur in young adulthood (the 20s and 30s) in the basic problem solving strategies used by the person in dealing with ethical issues. That is, the basic assumptions and perspectives by which people define what is morally right or wrong change in this period, and the change is just as dramatic and fundamental as change in the years before puberty. (1988, 23)

How this is to be achieved is also subject to some agreement. Researchers such as Rest and Muriel Bebeau, each of whom has experimented with moral education over a great many years, suggest that the moral education of adults is best achieved by presenting them with real case studies or scenarios relevant to adult experiences. In developing morally, adults learn to move from the particular, from specific instances of moral conflicts, to more general situations, seeking guidelines applicable to those and similar relationships. One begins by raising awareness of the existence of ethical issues, although raising awareness is not enough, by itself, to improve behavior. Additionally, Rest and Bebeau argue, one must provide students with moral reasoning skills to discuss, think through, and try to resolve the ethical issues illustrated in the cases. Through practice one becomes adept at analyzing particular cases and formulating more general decision procedures and principles to apply to new scenarios. Conversely, one could start from a general principle and apply it to a particular application. In a later section of this chapter I shall argue that beginning with general moral principles is usually not as successful as starting with particular cases, and in a later chapter I shall argue that the success of either sort of moral decision-making depends, in great part, on a well-functioning imagination (Bebeau, 1994; Rest, 1994; Rest and Naváez, 1994).

These movements, from the particular to the general and the converse, are illustrated differently in decisions of different companies. Earlier I mentioned the J&J Tylenol case. Led by its CEO, James Burke, J&J concluded that customers and customer relationships were the first priority, as stated in its credo. Although J&J had done nothing to cause the harm, the company permanently removed the Tylenol capsules from the market. Notice that in this instance human relationships, a particular set of relationships with customers, outweighed the fact that J&J had caused no harm. Because of the importance of customers and the company's relationship to them, J&J went beyond the demands of what it was causally responsible for.

In another case, we see principles driving particular decisions. Levi Strauss, long known as a very reputable company, recently began the process of pulling all its operations out of China. It decided to neither market, manufacture, nor sell products in that country and to halt the purchase of any raw materials, despite the potentially huge market for Levi jeans and other Levi Strauss products in China. The decision was made by the CEO, Robert Haas, against the recommendation of Levi Strauss's China Policy Group, a top management committee that had spent over a year debating the issue. The China Policy Group argued that, given the circumstances, Levi Strauss should continue to export raw materials from China and develop a manufacturing base in China while at the same time becoming an exemplar in China for the promotion of human rights and the proper treatment and pay for workers. However, Haas overrode that recommendation, citing the company's code of ethics, and proclaiming that

> [i]n countries that do not offer protection of basic legal and human rights, we potentially expose our employees who live and work there to unacceptable risks; and we subject the company to a claim of legitimizing and supporting governments whose practices are condemned. (April 27, 1993, cited in Katz and Paine, 1994, B3)

The discussion of theories of moral education helps us to understand the difference between the decision-making processes in these two cases. Both were ethical decisions taken after a great deal of thought. One might disagree with either decision on other ethical grounds. Actually, J&J was not liable for the Tylenol poisonings and thus did not have a moral responsibility for remedying that situation. Levi Strauss might have chosen the more morally risky path of developing its China market while trying to present a model for exemplary behavior and working to change China's human rights policies. Nevertheless, both companies tried to operate from a high stage of moral development, although each decision came at the problem at hand from a different perspective: J&J began with the primacy of particular relationships (those to its customers) and Levi Strauss with the primacy of human rights principles. In each case the decision-makers were dealing with the particular and the general, in J&J's case, the capsule crisis, long-term customer relationships, and their credo; in Levi Strauss's case general human rights principles, the fact of China's human rights violations, and the potentially large Chinese market. I shall argue later that it takes imagination, moral imagination, to make decisions such as these, because they go beyond apparent conventional demands of morality, of the market, or of the business in question.

In summary, moral development theories describe human cognitive and moral development. At least in part, they account for moral error and reiteration of mistakes, attributing these phenomena to lower stages of moral development. But theories of moral development have more difficulty explaining why an intelligent, well-educated person such as Jett, even if he is at a low stage of moral development, could get so involved in his job, his company, or himself that he would not perceive that he was very likely to get caught. Alternately, Jett may have been acting on a conventional level, responding to pressure from his past experiences and role expectations for traders at Kidder. But such an explanation assumes Jett's disregard for social convention and the law, again belying the expectations of that level of moral development. On any level of moral development, Jett has everything to lose by participating in this sort of trading. The moral development literature, then, does not go far enough in explaining why some managers and companies repeatedly engage in morally questionable behavior or are associated with untoward consequences. In the GE cases I have cited, the company could lose only when these situations went awry. There is no self-interested "payoff," either in the short run or long run, and little in the way of conventional explanation to account for these behaviors.

DESCRIPTIVE EXPLANATIONS

In every incident or set of events are a number of related common causes of the incident, factors that influence managerial and corporate behavior, any or all of which can cause the abdication of individual moral responsibility in corporate and other organizational settings. I shall discuss three: (1) the conflation of what is legal with what is expected morally, (2) an identification of professional responsibility with organizational responsibility, and (3) the identification of moral responsibility with role responsibility. I shall argue that each of these factors (and there are others) is important and necessary, indeed, crucial, to explaining the occurrence of events. However, none is sufficient to account completely for moral irresponsibility, nor is any sufficient to absolve managers and companies of moral culpability.

Let us take as a focus a 1993 *Wall Street Journal* article describing the details of the Ford Motor Company's development of its utility vehicle, the Bronco II:

> A prototype of Ford Motor Co.'s Bronco II lifted a front wheel off the road while rounding a test track in 1982. The lift-off was witnessed by the

company's head of automotive safety, his immediate superior and Ford's top in-house lawyer. The same day, Ford ordered supervising engineers to speed up the handing over to its lawyers of copies of all Bronco II engineering and safety records.

As it turned out, the lawyers' worries were prescient. After some safety-related revisions, the sporty Bronco II four-wheel drive went into production in January 1983, and a rear-wheel drive version $2\frac{1}{2}$ years later. By most measures, the vehicle, especially its rear-wheel drive version, was less stable than its main competitors' models. More than 260 people have died in accidents in which a Bronco II flipped over, according to the Insurance Institute for Highway Safety—several times more than with any similar vehicle.

Thus far, Ford has settled more than 100 lawsuits, all with strict confidentiality provisions, and has another 100 Bronco II cases pending.

The court records reveal that:

- Ford knew in 1981 that it could stabilize the vehicle considerably by switching to a much-wider chassis but, running behind in a race to market with General Motors Corp.'s S-10 Blazer, didn't do so.
- Faced later with evidence that the S-10 Blazer was going to hit the market with a better stability rating, Ford made mostly superficial last-minute changes in the Bronco II that proved to have little safety value.
- Tests that Ford ran after the Bronco II went on the market in 1983 continued to indicate the vehicle's tendency to tip or roll over on sharp turns. . . .

More than 50 documents that were supposed to be collected during the record-gathering couldn't be found when sought during pretrial fact-finding in the lawsuits. Ford officials say these documents were never turned over and were destroyed as part of routine records-management because of a misunderstanding among its engineers. Even a copy of the company manual for destroying records was destroyed.

Ford says its own studies show that the Bronco II is no less stable than some other sport utility vehicles in its class and that rollovers mostly result from other variables, such as poor road conditions and careless driving. And Ford defends its lawyers' role. . . .

In February 1989, the federal highway safety agency launched a recall investigation of the Bronco. . . . Ultimately, the agency decided not to take action because it concluded that it could point to no safety defect in the absence of a "component failure or malfunction."

Nonetheless, in June 1989, *Consumer Reports* criticized the Bronco II's performance in emergency-turn tests and photographed it tipping with two wheels in the air at 42 mph. "We think it's wise to avoid the Bronco II," the magazine cautioned. Ford criticized the test results as subjective, but by then it had already decided to pull out of the light utility market. (Geyelin and Templin, 1993, A1, 6)

Ford Motor Company, like GE, is often cited as one of the best-managed and economically successful companies in America (Collins and Porras, 1994). What led Ford, famous for having produced the Taurus as well as the Pinto, not to take fully into account the test results of the Bronco II? One interesting conjecture is that Ford determined that legality resolves moral issues. Companies such as Ford operate in a maze of legal and regulatory restrictions. In the Bronco II case, Ford brought in its top lawyer to watch the testing of Bronco II, and it did nothing illegal in producing this vehicle. Did Ford's executives, lawyers, engineers, and middle managers conclude that meeting government safety standards and keeping within the borders of the law absolved it of moral culpability for Bronco II? Did, Ford, in other words, depend on its legal experts to solve its moral problems?

A similar phenomenon occurred at Ford during the Pinto era. Between 1973 and 1975, a manager at Ford, Dennis Gioia, now professor of organizational behavior at Pennsylvania State University, was recall coordinator at Ford, in charge of recalls of defective automobiles. Gioia's job included identifying problems that might require a recall and organizing the recalls themselves. When a number of burned Pintos arrived back at Ford, Gioia became intimately familiar with the problems of the Pinto, yet he did not order a recall, he drove a Pinto, and he sold one to his sister. Gioia reports, "in the context of the times my actions were *legal* (they were all within the framework of the law). . . . [T]he major concern for me [retrospectively] is whether they were *moral* (in the sense of adhering to some higher standards of inner conscience and conviction about the 'right' actions to take)" (Gioia, 1991, 384). Gioia does not use this as a justification or as an excuse for his actions but merely as an explanation of why, at the time of his employment at Ford, neither he nor the other Ford managers questioned his actions. Only retrospectively, when Gioia began to examine his actions after he left Ford, was he able to distinguish between the legal and moral implications of the recall policy.

Connected to the conflation of legal and moral issues is a second factor that may affect managerial moral judgments. In making moral judgments, managers who are also members of professional organizations, for example, lawyers or engineers, must weigh their organizational responsibilities against their professional responsibilities. At least two kinds of professionals played key roles in the development of the Bronco II: engineers and lawyers. Both groups are members of professions that have codes of ethics. These codes proscribe the actions of these professionals just because they are members of those professions, and at least some of these code-proscriptions are meant to override both personal inclinations and nonprofessional organizational or corporate demands. As professionals, lawyers and engineers have strongly differentiated roles; that is, in cases of conflict, the demands of the professional role and its codes are supposed to override organizational, corporate, or other moral demands (Goldman, 1980, 2–4). "The American Bar Association's [ABA] Model Rules of Professional Conduct specifies that as advocate, a lawyer zealously asserts the client's position under the rules of the adversary system. . . . A lawyer should keep in confidence information relating to representation of a client"(Callahan, 1988, 439). At the same time, the ABA Model Rules states, "A lawyer shall not counsel a client to engage, or assist a client, in conduct that the lawyer knows is criminal or fraudulent"(Callahan, 1988, 440). Moreover,

> [a] lawyer may reveal [confidential] information to the extent the lawyer reasonably believes necessary to prevent the client from committing a criminal act that the lawyer believes is likely to result in imminent death or substantial bodily harm. . . . If a lawyer for an organization knows that an officer, employee or other person associated with the organization is engaged in action, intends to act or refuses to act in a matter related to the representation that is a violation of a legal obligation to the organization, or a violation of law which reasonably might be imputed to the organization, and is likely to result in substantial injury to the organization, the lawyer shall proceed as is reasonably necessary in the best interest of the organization. (Callahan, 1988, 441–2)

Given these professional guidelines, it is not clear that in defending Ford to the letter of the law, its lawyers acted within the guidelines of their profession, since it was scarcely in the best interest of Bronco II customers not to change the design. Eventually, too, Ford's long-term best interests were not served. Perhaps the identification of the legal with the moral interfered with a close examination of the *moral* proscriptions of the ABA professional code. Engineering codes specify that "'[e]ngineers in the fulfillment of their professional duties, shall: Hold paramount the safety, health and welfare of the public in the performance of their professional duties'" (Callahan, 1988, 460–1). Yet evidence suggests that engineers at Ford did not see the design of the Bronco II as a problem serious enough to warrant questioning its production. They may have missed the possibility of a conflict of interest between the demands of their professional code and those of their roles in Ford's production team. They appeared to allow organizational, Ford-defined role demands to dominate.

ROLES AND ROLE RESPONSIBILITIES

Ford's corporate culture decision dynamic may have clouded independent judgment of Ford's professionals. Ford's lawyers, engineers, and managers may have misidentified their role responsibilities, confusing the legal with the moral; conflated professional with managerial obligations; or identified role responsibilities with their moral responsibilities. Similarly, Joseph Jett, and perhaps, too, his bosses at Kidder, may have interpreted GE's CEO Jack Welch's edict to all his managers that every division at GE should be "No. 1 or No. 2 in every market it serves" (Tichy and Sherman, 1993, 72) as a prescription to do whatever was needed to make Kidder No. 1.

Let me qualify my arguments. It would certainly be a gross exaggeration and downright incorrect to say that a number of managers at Ford or at GE merely do as they are told and do not think for themselves as independent, morally responsible individuals. However, Ford, like other organizations, harbors some practices that neither encourage independent managerial decision-making nor provide avenues for questioning what might, by standards outside the institution, be unacceptable activities. Sometimes, too, managers become so involved in their roles and accompanying expectations that their judgments reflect what they perceive to be their role responsibilities.

A current example of this sort of behavior writ large is the case of MiniScribe. In 1985 MiniScribe was a young company that manufactured disk drives for personal computers. Its largest customer was IBM, but in the middle of that year IBM canceled its contract with MiniScribe. MiniScribe was flagged by a venture capital firm as a good investment, and one of MiniScribe's directors, Quentin Thomas Wiles, infused $20 million into MiniScribe and took over the management of the company. While pressuring his employees to succeed, Wiles reduced the work force by one fourth and reorganized the company more than a dozen times over a six-year period. In addition to being autocratic and intimidating, Wiles created sales objectives that could not be met. Faced with these demands, his managers and sales staff began shipping double orders to unwitting customers, manipulating inventory, and eventually even making up sales and accounts. Quality control became a low priority, and employees regularly shipped defective disk drives. At one point, according to some employees, when MiniScribe had run out of disk drives, they shipped bricks in the disk drive cartons (Zipser, 1989, A1, A8). According to another report, some employees broke into the outside auditor's car and altered auditors' reports; others created a "Cook Book" that instructed MiniScribe managers how to inflate financial results (Drake and Peavy, 1995, 68–73). What is most disturbing is that at least 60 managers and employees condoned this scheme and participated in this behavior for over six years, even though they had to know that it was wrong. They seemed so absorbed in their role responsibilities to meet Wiles's sales projections or to keep their jobs that they simply lost perspective. They just followed orders, violating another role responsibility: to do one's job well—in this case, to produce, market, and ship quality disk drives, and to serve customers.[3]

I have used MiniScribe to dramatize two simple and common phenomena: the confusion of role responsibilities to do one's job well with the role responsibility to follow management orders, and second, the subordination of concern with more general moral responsibilities to those of one's role. Each of us functions within a political system, within social and economic institutions, in a culture, under law, and connected to a set of religious, cultural, and social mores. Sometimes, even if one grasps the right action, one is prevented, or appears to be prevented, from executing that action by regulation, law, custom, sanctions, or other pressures. The MiniScribe factor works on a number of levels. A corporate culture, a set of regulations, a government, law, religious convictions, peer pressures, or even personal habits can entrap individuals or groups of individuals in a perspective that is either ultimately self-defeating or self-deceptive. The MiniScribe managers' contentions that they were "just following orders," or "doing their job," illustrate in a dramatic way that entrapment.

Let us step back from these examples to define "role" and role morality. Role

> refer[s] to constellations of institutionally specified rights and duties organized around an institutionally specified social function . . . [where] an institution [is any public system or social arrangement that] includes rules that define offices and positions which can be occupied by different individuals at different times. (Hardimon, 1994, 334–5)

Families (however defined), professions, trades and trade unions, corporations, churches, and states are all institutions. Not all social arrangements entail roles. For example, friendships may not involve role differentiation, and, depending on the cultural context, characteristics such as race and gender may or may not have social role dimensions. Everyone in every society has a number of roles that define various relationships between individuals, between individuals and institutions, and between institutions themselves. Each of us as an individual has a large number of interacting and overlapping cultural, professional, religious, and social roles, and these change. For example, I am of Irish background, a mother, a daughter, a professor, a writer, a student, a consultant, an employee, an employer, a Protestant, an American, a member of the world community, an environmentalist, a liberal, a humanist, and so on. All of these adjectives describe intricate social relationships, and some of them refer to my social roles.

Roles have an impersonal quality. They are general descriptions or refer to a social status, such as motherhood, that apply to all occupants of that role, or at least, occupants of that role within a particular culture, ethnic group, or profession. Roles carry with them certain expectations, rights and duties, norms, and ideals that are either implicit or explicit, even sometimes legally or contractually defined. There is an impersonal, socially defined collection of expectations and demands that comes with each role, and when we take on a role we assume certain rights and duties as we "play the role." Connected, for example, with the role of an engineer are certain technical expectations connected with that role, job expectations depending on the engineer's position, and as a member of a profession, certain professional normative demands. In addition, most roles are usually associated with ideals, norms that define, for example, the perfect mother or the ideal firefighter (Downie, 1971; Emmet, 1966; Hardimon, 1994; Luben, 1988; Werhane, 1985). Thus, along with each role are moral demands as spelled out by that role, and these define what David Luben has called "role morality" (Andre, 1991; Luben, 1988, chapter 6).

That we have roles, that there are certain expectations in occupying these roles that most of us adhere to most of the time, and that we make moral judgments about role behavior are crucial elements of human experience and social interrelationships. The existence of roles permits a predictability of human behavior and a stability in social relationships. Ordinarily there are good moral reasons for acting according to role demands and ideals. A mother who ignores her children or a manager who does not take seriously his fiduciary responsibilities to his company under most circumstances is judged to be immoral both by the standards of role morality and by judgment of a common sense perspective (Andre, 1991).

The difficulty is that each of us is enmeshed in a collection of overlapping social, professional, cultural, and religious roles, each of which makes moral demands. This condition becomes problematic when the demands of a particular role become confused, when these demands come into conflict with those of another role, or when role demands clash with what we might call common morality. The lawyer who protects a known repeated murderer, the psychologist or priest who honors the confidentiality of a criminal's confession, or the reporter who witnesses a spouse committing a crime faces role conflicts. They are pulled in different directions by their professions, their personal ties, perhaps the company where they work or the partnership to which they belong, and commonly held societal moral norms. In business, as both the Bronco II and J&J cases illustrate, albeit with different consequences, the managerial role pressure to be competitive, efficient, and profitable can often conflict with the claims of common morality.

Sometimes we adopt two or more contradictory roles simultaneously without perceiving possible conflicts of interest. The most obvious examples are members of the US crime syndicate who are often exemplary church members and good family persons, and yet use a decision model in business dealings that contradicts the values of church and family. "Mafia mentality," as I would crudely label this phenomenon, is the ability to function in such contradictory roles simultaneously. This phenomenon is not limited to criminal activities. Take, for instance, the famous Lockheed Aircraft extortion scandal in the 1970s. In 1972 Lockheed, a company then in deep financial trouble, was trying to get a contract for its TriStar passenger airplane with a Japanese airline. Eventually, after paying approximately $12 million dollars in secret extortion payments, payments which, as it turned out, went to officials of the Japanese government (who later were convicted and went to jail), Lockheed received the contract. In assessing the decision, Lockheed's president at the time, Carl Kotchian, explained how he was *personally* "disgusted" with the arrangement. But the payments did not violate American law at that time, and as CEO of a company that might have gone under without the TriStar contract, his role demanded that the payments be authorized and made (Kotchian, 1977, 7–12).

Kotchian perceived his commitment to Lockheed's survival as defining a strongly differentiated role, one whose demands take precedence over other moral commitments (Goldman, 1980, 2–4). Ordinarily we reserve the notion of a strongly differentiated role to describe professionals such as doctors, nurses, lawyers, or engineers whose autonomous professional codes dictate certain forms of behavior that take precedence when one faces choices that invite ignoring the professional code in question. Managers are thought to have weakly differentiated roles because there is no independent professional managerial code that sets standards for professional managerial behavior. Yet Kotchian saw himself as a Lockheed executive first; his personal morality was put on hold while he made the decision to participate in the extortion scheme.

There is another kind of problem with role morality. Acting within the normative expectations of one's role cannot always be guaranteed to produce the best outcomes. On the night before the 1986 *Challenger* explosion, which I will discuss in the next chapter, engineers and managers at Morton Thiokol, the maker of the O-rings now known to be the cause of the explosion, found themselves in disagreement about whether to launch the *Challenger,* a disagreement that, in part, was due to their conflicting roles. A number of the engineers on the project at Thiokol protested the launch because of the impending bad weather, including low temperatures and high winds predicted for the next morning. The engineers cited three factors in their protest. First, there would be considerable difficulty retrieving the shuttle boosters after the launch in choppy sea waters. Second, ice in the booster support troughs might affect the shuttle orbiter. Third, they could not predict the behavior of the O-rings that sealed the booster joints, because the O-rings had not been tested at temperatures below 50 degrees (Fahrenheit) (the weather prediction was for about 30 degrees for scheduled launch). The engineers saw themselves in two important roles. First, as members of the engineering profession, their first responsibility was to safety. Second, as engineers, they held the scientific conviction that if a phenomenon has not been tested, one cannot presume a mechanism will work; indeed, the engineering assumption is usually that without proof of safety one cannot conclude that the mechanism will not fail (*Report,* 1986).

In contradistinction, the managers at Thiokol might have seen themselves in different roles and thus evaluated data differently. Their first priority was to execute the launch. Because there had been 24 previously successful launches, their conclusion was that this one had a great chance of success. Moreover, given such short notice, the engineers could not prove that the O-rings and shuttle orbiters would *not* function at temperatures below 50 degrees, nor could the engineers verify that the boosters could *not* be recovered in high seas, for the procedure had never been tested. From these premises, the managers at Thiokol concluded that all would go well. Hence, the managers seemed to have concluded that the O-rings had functioned in the past; if engineers cannot prove they will fail this time, they will work. Thiokol's managers failed to understand the engineers' point of view, one of the senior managers overrode the engineers' protest, and Thiokol signed off on the launch (Messick and Bazerman, 1996; Werhane, 1991b).

The engineers at Thiokol who protested the launch did not "blow the whistle" before the launch took place, either to top management at Morton Thiokol or at NASA, perhaps because they saw their roles as providers of data but without power as the final decision-makers. In the *Challenger* disaster, all these people were well meaning, all were acting within the normative expectations of their roles, and the *Challenger* exploded. (Vaughn, 1996; Werhane, 1991b).

Individuals are identified in a nexus of social roles and social relationships. By analogy, organizations such as corporations define themselves in terms of their roles as spelled out in their objectives. The roles of corporations are related to their function, their mission, and their goals. As with individuals, we hold corporations morally responsible for carrying out their role responsibilities. When the baby food manufacturer Beech-Nut some years ago was found to make apple juice that contained almost no apple juice, it was held liable for that oversight (Halliday and Paine, 1992). Similarly, Union Carbide has been held responsible for the Bhopal disaster because, it is argued, it was within the expectations of its role responsibilities as manufacturers of dangerous chemicals to have instituted safety measures that would have prevented this accident.

We sometimes hold companies responsible for untoward consequences of their actions even when at first sight they appear not to be within their role responsibilities. For example, the media has excoriated H. B. Fuller because the glue it manufactures in Honduras, Resistal, is sniffed by Honduran street children as a drug, and the glue-sniffing street children are called "Resistaleros." Yet Fuller argues that it is making glue, not drugs, it sells glue only in large containers to wholesalers, and children sniff many kinds of glue. The company's glue is repackaged and sold to children, but not because of any action Fuller had taken (Bowie and Lenway, 1993).

What is to be learned from the discussion of roles and role morality? First, and most obviously, roles function normatively, and we react to their responsibilities and demands. Beech-Nut was responsible for its apple juice manufacture because that was what it was in business to do. MiniScribe was responsible for producing and sending out reliable disk drives. These companies' roles are clear in these cases, and role morality is important in sorting out normative demands of each role and providing criteria for evaluative judgments.

However, role morality presents some other challenges. The observers of Bronco II testing were acting as agents for Ford, and deliberately so, but they may have violated their professional codes. And what about the roles of Beech-Nut and MiniScribe managers? The Beech-Nut case is a clear incident of corporate role violation; the difficulty is in explaining why any manager at the company supplying Beech-Nut with its juice concentrate thought that not including apple juice in apple juice concentrate was appropriate. At Beech-Nut and MiniScribe, was the managers' primary responsibility to produce reliable apple juice and disk drives, or was their first priority to obey the directions of top management? In each of these incidents, managers faced conflicting role responsibilities—to be good managers or good professionals, or to be obedient managers and disobedient professionals. To settle these conflicts, one cannot appeal merely to role morality, because it is the moral demands of each role that are at issue.

There is a second shortcoming of role morality. While role responsibilities account for much of what we do, and role morality is important in judging accountability for role responsibilities, not all moral responsibility can be reduced to role responsibility or even to the question of conflicting role responsibilities. In the *Challenger* explosion, for example, each person, each manager, and each engineer acted within the ordinary guidelines of his or her role or profession, with dreadful consequences.

We tend to judge people in their roles not merely by the demands of that role or by conflicting demands as in the MiniScribe case, but also by the demands of common morality. Our evaluation of Adolph Eichmann is one very strong example. Eichmann was an exemplary clerk and a law-abiding citizen. But that is not enough, in itself, to excuse his behavior. We do not want to let him off the "moral hook," so to speak, despite his "proper" behavior, his efficiency, and patriotic commitment. We want to say that what he did was wrong and evil *because* he so completely identified with his role, his station, and its duties, and because of the terrible consequences of his role actions.

The Eichmann and MiniScribe examples bring up the most dangerous difficulty with role adaptation and role morality, that of unquestioned obedience to one's role demands, particularly when those demands are defined by a person or an institution in authority. Beginning in 1964, Stanley Milgram, a psychologist, carried out a set of experiments that demonstrated how individuals, when given a set of instructions by a person in authority, will often carry out those instructions, even when they are absurd, dangerous, or life-threatening. In the Milgram experiments the subject was asked to give an electric shock to what he or she was told was an innocent learner if the learner did not respond correctly to some fairly innocuous questions. With each mistake the learner received an increasingly intense shock, up to 450 volts. If a subject questioned the experiment or expressed concern about inflicting electric shock on the learner, who was a stranger to the subject, an authority figure in a white coat, often Milgram himself, assured the subject that he or she was following a documented scientific procedure, and that "the experiment must go on." Some subjects simply quit in the middle of the process, yet in experiment after experiment, Milgram and his students were surprised to discover that over 50% of all subjects carried out the shock level to the 450 volts. Although the experiment was set up so that the learner did not actually receive real shocks, the subjects did not know that until after the experiment was completed (Milgram, 1969).

In a later experiment, Philip Zimbardo (1973) conducted an experiment with college students, many of whom had read Milgram's work. In Zimbardo's experiments students were to act out prison roles as wardens, guards, or prisoners over a period of two weeks. Prison-like cells were created and role-playing student "prisoners" were "arrested" and brought to the "prison." After a few days most of the prisoners became subservient to the "guards," and the guards in turn became aggressive, dominating, and in some cases inflicted arbitrary punishment. Zimbardo had to abort the experiment after six days because of the inhumane treatment of prisoners by the guards. Playing a role or acting under conditions that are defined and shaped by an authority figure, then, Milgram and Zimbardo concluded, can produce unthinkable consequences.

While less dramatic, many MiniScribe managers followed the whims of Wiles or what they perceived to be his directives even when their actions became illegal, nonsensical, and just silly. Thus, in certain circumstances role demands can override ordinary, common sense moral sensitivity or smother individual conscience (Arendt, 1963; Wicks and Freeman, 1990).

How do we account for moral blameworthiness in these examples so that moral judgments about role behavior are not confined to whether an agent is fulfilling his or her role? In this context, it is tempting to conclude that the object of the moral judgment is the self apart from its roles, the self as an independent moral agent, not merely the self as it is engaged in its roles, a self that is both free from identification with any particular role and is ultimately, because of its autonomy, morally responsible. It is *that* self we are holding morally responsible when we condemn Eichmann for following his role responsibilities, and it is that group of selves we hold morally accountable at Beech-Nut for eliminating apples in apple juice.

Because each of us has many roles and because we are capable of distancing ourselves from any one role, we need not be fully engaged in any one role so that it becomes overriding. Each of us has a variety of roles and role responsibilities; no one role completely defines the self. Moreover, no person is so mired in one role that he or she cannot be distant from its demands, even though we often fail to do so. Even as children we learn to play and play-act various roles. We learn early on about distancing ourselves from identifying completely with any one particular role. Each of us can compare and contrast various roles and role responsibilities simply because no one role is complete and because we have so many of them (Goffman, 1961 92–5).

But what is the nature of the non-role-defined self—the moral agent to whom we ascribe moral responsibilities as distinguished from role responsibilities? When one attempts to sort out the self apart from its roles, there is a further difficulty—the difficulty of getting at that self. When I eliminate all my roles, as professor, mother, daughter, sister, writer, citizen, environmentalist, humanist, Democrat, what is left? Who I am is created in large measure from these roles. Roles and role morality overlap with other social relationships so that the division is not always clear. This is evident in citizenship, for example, where duties are less well defined and where one's role could be sharply or vaguely differentiated. All I have left without my roles are vague social relationships. I am now a friend without role duties, a distant relative, a nonvoting American, a person of Irish descent, a nonpracticing Protestant, an observer, a reader, an appreciator but not a critic of art, and so on. Without any roles I become more amorphous, less defined, and it is difficult to delineate my responsibilities and obligations as a moral person.

Without roles we are left with the quandary of how to relate moral agency to moral responsibility. Moreover, even without roles, a notion of the self, Michael Sandel and others argue, cannot be purely autonomous or devoid of *all* social relationships without being what Sandel has called "dispossessed," and indeed, altogether empty. In *A Theory of Justice* (1971), John Rawls argues that principles of justice are best constructed by rational persons behind a hypothetical "veil of ignorance" where individuals have no knowledge of their place in history; their cultural, ethnic, religious, or economic circumstances; their social status; or even their age, gender, intelligence, or natural abilities. From this position individuals have no knowledge of their own emotions, desires, value system, or of their place in history or society. Rawls argues that postulating this hypothetical position is necessary in order to draw up principles of justice that will be fair to people whatever their position, social or economic status, gender, religion, ethnic background, or historical position. Hypothetically, this would be the position of an ideal spectator, one who was totally disengaged from his or her community and life circumstances, an individual who, then, at least according to Rawls and others who hold this view, could make purely disinterested moral judgments and develop universal principles of justice and morality. Such a person would be at Kohlberg's highest stage of moral development.

Michael Sandel persuasively claims, however, that individuals in such a position would be "wholly unencumbered subjects" (1982, 172) and thus devoid of character and the ability to make worthwhile choices. If I disengage myself from all my roles and social relationships, I become ahistorical, without family, gender, nationality, ethnicity, and cultural perspective. Thus, I become devoid of desires, values, and goals; I become psychologically empty. Having no background and no possibilities (or every possibility) from which to choose, individuals behind a veil of ignorance simply make blind choices on the basis of "arbitrarily-given preferences" (Sandel, 1982, 168). In that case the notion of autonomy makes no sense because as a purely autonomous self one is without psychological resources to form choices, to accept or reject alternatives, or to make moral judgments. Such a self can be neither responsible nor irresponsible because it has no resources with which to make judgments at all, and principles it adapts would be equally arbitrary (Luben, 1988, 122–30; Sandel, 1982, 154–74).

On the other hand, if the self is merely determined by its various socially defined roles and social relationships, it is "radically situated" so that its actions merely result from the complex interrelationships between these roles. If this is the sum total of who we are, it is not easy to explain how we are self-reflective, self-critical, creative makers of history and authors of change. Nor can that description account fully for moral blame. As a result, we would be forced to conclude that Eichmann was simply a product of the Third Reich and thus exempt from further moral condemnation. Whereas Beech-Nut itself is morally blameworthy for not fulfilling its role as a manufacturer of baby food, its managers were simply following orders. Most of us are uneasy with this conclusion, but without *some* notion of an autonomous self, it is difficult to formulate an explanation of what appears to be one's ability to choose, change, and deal with role conflicts, and thus be subject to moral judgment. What we want to say is that the moral agent we attempt to hold responsible for role behavior is always an engaged agent-self, not an abstract dispossessed entity, but one not merely determined by social relationships and roles—something more than one's engagements.

In defending the view that "the self is socially constructed," Larry May, following Charles Taylor, argues that what we call the self or personal identity of the self is a "web knit from various identifications and commitments that one makes with various social groups" (May, 1996, 13). A large part of that web, I would argue, consists of one's roles. Out of this web, one develops a core, according to May, a sense of self-identity formed and made up from commitments and values integrated in this web of relationships. The uniqueness of each self is formed from the peculiar web of roles and relationships one develops out of social interactions. As we mature, one can develop a sense of stability and integrity that creates a temporary unity of the core self, but still, the core self is by and large a self-in-process.

May has carefully advanced the notion of a socially constructed self; still, if the core self is a nexus of roles and relationships, one is left with questions concerning the nature of the moral self that we hold responsible despite its roles and relationships, because how or whether the core self is something more than its web of commitments and relationships is unclear.

David Luben attempts to solve the problem of the moral self that is more than its roles and relationships by arguing that, in making moral judgments about role responsibilities, we acknowledge each other as persons subject to precepts of common morality. At the same time, individually and personally, we cannot get at the self within us that is an utterly independent autonomous agent *except* as a nexus of roles. Luben is mostly correct in the following remarks:

> Ultimately, we reserve our autonomy from our stations and their duties so that we have the freedom to respond to persons *qua* persons—to obey what one may call the *morality of acknowledgment.* The situation is curiously asymmetrical: we are bound to extend to others a courtesy we are bound to refuse to ourselves. It is a delusion to think of *myself* as just a person *qua* person, a "me" outside of my social station[s]; but when the chips are down, it is immoral to think of you as anything less. (1988, 127)

There are, however, two problems with Luben's conclusion. First, Luben tends to assume that a human being is merely the sum of roles, or at least, that all human relationships are role relationships. I think, however, there is more to be said about the person qua person who is myself. Although it is true that we cannot divorce ourselves from our relationships, the fact that we can get at a distance from any particular role implies an act of a self not merely a sum of its roles and social relationships.

In his book *Thick and Thin* (1994), Michael Walzer tries to account for a notion of moral agency that avoids both the difficulties of proposing a radically situated social self and the metaphysical problems of postulating a purely autonomous or dispossessed self. To achieve this, Walzer distinguishes "thick" and "thin" aspects of the self. If I understand his position correctly, Walzer claims that all our experiences are socially derived, perspectival, and constructed from our social, historical situation and its accompanying narratives. In that socialization process, we develop a number of interests, roles, memberships, commitments, and values such that each individual is an historical, cultural, and social product, a pluralistic bundle of overlapping spheres of foci, a thick self or selves. In the first instance, there is no self as a precritical, transcendental subject, totally ideal spectator, or dispossessed subject. Self-reflection and self-criticism develop but only later out of the thick socialized self or bundle of selves. Who we are as subjects of these experiences is a late development from our socialization process. Self-reflection arises when there are inconsistencies, disagreements, or clashes between one's interests, roles, commitments, and values, clashes that jar one into taking another point of view, a "meta" point of view that is still one's own. This view develops when one judges and redirects one's interests, choices, and commitments, and when one sees oneself in historical/social continuity and as a unity of thick perspectives. Walzer calls this point of view the thin aspect of the self. The thin self accounts for the unity and continuity of overlapping, changing thick selves and for our ability to make choices and changes that are not merely outcomes of our roles and social situation. Walzer, borrowing from Lionel Trilling, claims that this thin self "perdures" (Trilling, 1972, 99; Walzer, 1994, 101) through time and change. Yet, although it perdures, thus accounting for self-identity, the self is no more than the unity of a bundle of social selves, the self-reflective locus of this vast array of experiences. The thin self, then, is socially derived but not merely socially determined. It accounts for one's ability to choose, manipulate, and even change events, and it explains our ability to get a perspective on our situation and its positive and negative features. The self that is the role-evaluator, and that same self I hold morally responsible for its role behavior, is a thin self, that which is the locus of the thick self, the self engaged in, defined and changed by, and changing, its various roles (Walzer, 1994, chapter 5).

The second shortcoming of Luben's conclusion is his assumption that the morality of acknowledgment is asymmetrical. That is, according to Luben, I recognize that others are moral persons, but I cannot acknowledge that personhood of or in myself, because I cannot perceive or get at the self apart from its roles and relationships. Appealing to the work of Emmanuel Levinas (1979), however, one can develop a viable response to Luben's conclusion. Even if we cannot get at the self apart from these roles and relationships, the act of recognizing others as persons is a reciprocal experience. Levinas says that in confronting other people in moral dialogue where we acknowledge others as moral selves, we acknowledge others as more than their roles and relationships. This confrontation or series of confrontations is often reciprocal in the sense that we perceive that other people perceive or acknowledge us as more than our roles and relationships. That is, in Walzer's terms, we both see others as thin as well as thick selves, and we recognize that others perceive us similarly. Although this reciprocal acknowledgement may not be a dramatic as Levinas depicts it, it is surely the case that when we recognize and treat others as persons qua persons, we expect and indeed, demand, reciprocal respect. Those exchanges between persons give me an understanding of myself as a moral agent despite my inability to isolate that phenomenon, because I see myself through its reflection in the way others treat me and create expectations about my behavior that often transcend role expectations. It is in those exchanges where I treat others as persons and where I recognize another person's consideration and judgment of myself as a person that I recognize myself as a moral agent. In acknowledging others as moral agents, I realize that I am more than my roles, even though I cannot perceive and have difficulty getting at the "more"—the pure subject self—without a loss of the sense of self altogether (Levinas, 1979; Werhane, 1997).

Returning to the question of role morality and moral responsibility, one may conclude from this discussion that (1) the identification of legal and moral responsibility, (2) the priority of institutional or managerial demands over professional codes and other moral demands, (3) the demands of obedience to one's role expectations, and (4) role morality explain, at least in part, why good managers and good companies engage in questionable behavior. But role morality does not explain all moral or immoral behavior or offer avenues for resolving conflicts of interest or settling professional or legal dilemmas.

Because as human beings we are not exhaustively defined by our roles, each of us can get at a distance from and evaluate our roles and role responsibilities. Tools for evaluation include appeals to the precepts of common morality, those rules or precepts that most of us, stepping out of our roles and judging others, would regard as guides for how we and others ought to behave (moral rules such as equal respect for persons, avoidance of harm, respect for rights and fairness, honoring contracts, and respect for property), however particularly defined. Moreover, as Luben carefully asserts, we can and should use those same tools of common morality for judging organizations and institutions, particularly one's own organizations. Just as we evaluate people, we can also assess organizations and institutions, their roles, and the ends they allegedly serve. According to Luben, then, we can evaluate any role, its role-defined obligations, the organization to which it is attached, and whatever acts the role, role duties, or organization seem to demand. At each step we evaluate the role, role obligations, and the organization or institution both in terms of what justifies the institution, role, obligation, or act, and what the organization, role, obligation, or act justifies (Luben, 1988, chapters 6 and 7).

For example, if one is asked to shred documents on the Bronco II trial test runs, (assuming one's job is shredder), one examines one's role and role obligations first in terms of what justifies the institutions and organizations in question, in this case, free enterprise, auto manufacture, and Ford, the company. At this point one might argue that business corporations are justified as socioeconomic organizations if they in fact improve well-being (e.g., by providing jobs, goods, and services), or at least if they do not contribute to reducing economic benefits; if they are good corporate citizens or at least, not bad citizens; if they do not violate basic human rights; and if they do not create a net balance of harms in their activities. Then, one would ask, does the well-being of Ford justify producing a flawed automobile that could be altered without undue cost to the company or its customers? Does my role as an employee of Ford override my role as shredder, or is my role as shredder so important that it overrides the value of what it is shredding (e.g., documents that verify Bronco II's rollover problems)?

Obviously, it is difficult to evaluate every action one takes in every role without becoming consumed with evaluation as a full-time activity, and, as I shall argue in chapter 3, there are limits to one's impartiality and disengagement. But the act of stepping out of one's role and creating a distance from its obligations and the organization in which the role operates can put into perspective the relative importance of the organization and its role demands. Such steps of evaluation are crucial, I would conclude, to avoid problems such as Joseph Jett found himself embroiled in, and on the corporate level, to avoid the postproduction problems with Bronco II, or Beech-Nut's "apple" juice. It is those very steps that James Burke took in pulling Tylenol capsules off the market and Robert Haas instigated at Levi Strauss to pull out of the China market.

TRAINING IN MORAL REASONING

There is another temptation in trying to answer why good people or fine institutions engage in questionable behavior or why we repeat our mistakes. This temptation is to argue that the missing element in the cases I cited in chapter 1 and in this chapter is managerial skill in moral reasoning. Given the failure of descriptive pathologies to prevent moral aphasia, the limits of role morality, and complications in arguing that managers are primarily motivated by self-interest or even greed, one confronts a fourth temptation: to improve moral behavior through traditional moral education. Managers at Ford, GE, GM, Union Carbide, and elsewhere are rational adults who are responsible, morally responsible, for the engineering, legal and marketing decisions, and production of Pinto, Bronco II, full-sized pickups, the Bhopal plant, Kidder's bond trading, and so on. So, this argument continues, let us talk to the managers of these companies about professional and moral responsibilities through the introduction of moral theory, locate the managers who misbehaved, and begin moral education. We might then test their stage of moral development and give them workshops on moral reasoning. That is, are they egoists, conformists, rule followers, law abiders, precedent setters, or philosophers? We will discuss professional and organizational codes of ethics, demonstrate the limits of role responsibilities and role morality, present some ethical theories (e.g., utilitarianism, deontology, virtue theory), and some theories of justice, and engage these managers in a series of practice sessions that apply moral theories to cases studies.

Recalling our discussion of the self in the last section, one might be tempted to link a notion of the thin self to impartiality, and that in turn to rational moral decision-making, and then to argue that an impartial rational perspective from which one engages in a moral reasoning process will solve or avoid many of the problems I have cited. The Ford and GE scenarios, in particular, suggest that one needs to find distance from the organization and its decision-making habits. A less biased perspective is crucial, because unless a manager can disengage from the context of a specific problem and his or her role in that problem, and unless an organization can do so also, parochially embedded decisions will result in activities that invite repeated moral failure. Scenarios such as phantom trading repeat themselves when one is unable to view one's role, one's company, and their demands from a more general moral perspective.

Therein lies the problem. Lawyers and engineers are bound by professional codes of ethics; still, questionable activities persist in these professions. Most of the *Fortune* 1000 companies in the United States have codes of ethics, credos, or mission statements. At least one third of them have ethics officers and ethics programs in place (Kamm, 1993). Yet improprieties continue even in companies such as GE with its strong code of ethics and a well-developed ethics program for its managers.

The difficulty is not that moral principles are wrongheaded or that morality reduces to role morality. The difficulty is that when one begins from the general, starting with moral theory or theories, and then applies these theories or generalities to particular cases, sometimes there is a disconnect between theory and practice. This move is analogous to beginning with a discussion of the thin self without recognizing that it is an outcome of a nexus of thick social relationships. If Sandel is right, this discussion would be, at best, brief, because one cannot get at the thin self except through the thickness of its relationships and social context. Thus, Rest and others assert that ethics teaching begins with the particular—with particular cases or scenarios that capture the imagination from which one then generalizes. Moral decision-making should begin with particular real cases and scenarios, because that is what engages our interest, emotions, and moral sentiments. I would argue that the subject matter of morality is the real—particular actual cases, characters, events, situations, and dilemmas—the "thick" of human experience. Moral theory is about those cases. To begin with abstract moral theory separates that theory from the particular in such a way as to create two apparently separate realms of discourse. The disconnect between theory and practice is created in part because moral theory is formal or general, not contextual. Applications make sense only after terms have been defined to fit the situation. For example, some formulations of the principle of utility state that the end of morality and the proper goal of all moral action is to create "the greatest happiness for the greatest number" (e.g., Bentham, 1789/1948). But the term happiness is abstract. When one defines it, one uses particular illustrations relative to particular persons or contexts so that the allegedly universal utilitarian formula is no longer universally applicable. Even virtue theory, which sometimes claims to be more situational, has difficulty if one begins by discussing the virtues, say, of courage or excellence, outside of a context. Courage in war, for example, is (or should be) different from courage in business.

In chapters 3 and 5 I shall argue that all experience is socially structured, all experience is interpreted, so, as Martha Nussbaum has noted, "moral experience is an interpretation of the seen" (1990, 130). Some moral theorists try to distance themselves from that conclusion, but formal moral principles themselves are interpretations or constructions that also serve as framing mechanisms for the phenomena of our experience. Hence, if we look at some cases, such as the Lockheed sale of TriStars to Japan, from a utilitarian perspective, we could plausibly conclude that the small percentage of total sales accounted for in the extortion paid to the Japanese was worth the long-term benefit to the company and its employees and shareholders. If we look at the case from a more Kantian perspective, worrying about the questionability and negative precedent-setting nature of extortion, we might well come to another conclusion. These different ethical theories frame the case in contrasting ways so as to create different and sometimes even contradictory conclusions. This does not happen in every scenario, but that it happens in a number of instances illustrates how a particular ethical theory itself frames our experiences and how different theory frames the same experience differently. This phenomenon gives cause to worry about the efficacy of beginning with ethical theory in working through issues in business ethics.

There is an attendant problem, a problem with "limited rationality." It is possible within a particular institutional or theoretical context to develop limited objectivity so as to create a closed loop of decision-making. The Nestlé Corporation produces some of the finest infant formula in the world. It is an international company with excellent products, superb marketing skills, and a code of ethics. In selling infant formula worldwide Nestlé was successful in a number of markets including Europe, North America, and Asia. In particular, in Singapore, it claims to have saved thousands of lives of infants whose mothers could not nurse their babies.

From one perspective, given these facts it seems reasonable to take the same product, the same marketing plans, and the same communication techniques to market infant formula in new countries. From a utilitarian perspective, too, this approach seems to be the right thing to do, all things considered. So Nestlé began marketing infant formula in East Africa, using textbook and tested general marketing principles that had been successful in a number of markets. The result has been the deaths of hundreds of thousands of infants as a direct result of being taken off breast milk. What went wrong (Sethi, 1994)?

In this new environment Nestlé failed to take into account a new context, a context in which most customers cannot read directions on the formula labels, where clean water to mix the formula is nonexistent, and where the poverty level is so high that mothers overdiluted the formula, thus starving their children. Moreover, Nestlé failed to realize that some cultures frame their experiences differently than others. In a number of tribes in East Africa, medicine men are thought of as gods. When men in white coats promote infant formula, thousands of mothers thought it was their duty to feed it to their children. Thus, what appeared to be reasonable and indeed a proper marketing approach failed because Nestlé did not take into account traditions of African cultures or the religious conceptual scheme through which an East African mother projects her experiences, or the level of poverty and ecology in these countries (Sethi, 1994). This suggests that what appears to be a rational perspective, while crucial to moral decision-making, may create a disconnect between what appears *in theory* to be correct and what, in particular fact, is so. I am suggesting that what seems to be a rational perspective, simply applying rules, for example, well-tested marketing principles and techniques, to a new situation may not be enough, by itself, to avoid moral disasters.

Nestlé was universally highly criticized for this marketing scheme and its practices were condemned by WHO. Hundreds of moral philosophers wrote papers on how Nestlé had ignored moral rules and flaunted human rights in carrying out these activities. Interestingly, however, Nestlé ignored these diatribes, not understanding the application of moral principles to this case, arguing that there was nothing wrong with the formula. That was true; the infant formula is a great product. What was wrong was that Nestlé's principled marketing techniques did not function adequately in the context of developing African countries. The company ignored the second principle of marketing: "know your customer."

Interestingly, while operating by applying the general (marketing principles) to the particular (East Africa), Nestlé seemed unable to integrate the normative proscriptions of morality into these particular sets of actions; that is, Nestlé seemed unable to apply general principles to this particular. Only when a US boycott of Nestlé food products produced a 40% reduction in the US market share, did Nestlé reform its marketing practices in East Africa. Nestlé understood that particular very well (Sethi, 1994).

CONCLUSION

We have before us, then, a number of factors that may contribute to morally questionable behavior and to repeatability of that behavior in similar circumstances. Self-interest, greed, and retarded moral development may be contributing phenomena. A confusion of legal and moral demands, possible conflicts of interest between professional and institutional commitments, conflicts of role responsibilities, or the identification of moral responsibility with role responsibility may lead to the subsequent abdication of individual moral responsibility to organizational demands. Analyses such as these are helpful in pinpointing weaknesses in individual, managerial, and corporate decision-making. But such analyses do not successfully attack the problem of moral lapses. Since the price-fixing scandals of the 1950s, GE has repeatedly been involved in newsworthy morally questionable activities. Ford was subject to careful, exhaustive public scrutiny after the Pinto problems, yet Bronco II was put into production without design changes.

Apparently at least two factors are missing at these companies. Many of these managers and their organizations appear to lack (1) the ability to step back from their situation, to look at their roles, decisions, and actions from another perspective to evaluate or reassess their activities, and (2) a modicum of moral imagination, that is, the ability to imagine a wider range of possible issues, consequences, and remedies (e.g., that manufacturing the Bronco II might be a problem, that phantom trading might be questionable, or that the Pentagon might get tired of violations of military contracts). In some instances companies have not challenged themselves, in the ways Levi Strauss and J&J have, to find out whether there might be another viable and profitable way to conduct business. In the chapters to follow I will explore these options.

3

"The Very Idea of a Conceptual Scheme"

On January 28, 1986, within a minute after liftoff, the *Challenger* space shuttle exploded in midair, killing all on board including the first schoolteacher to go into space. Morton Thiokol, a company formed by the acquisition of Thiokol by the Morton Salt Company, was the manufacturer of the solid fuel rocket boosters for the space shuttle program, including the boosters for the ill-fated *Challenger*.[1] The *Challenger* explosion has been traced to the failure of the O-rings, the seals in the connecting joint between two segments of the rocket booster, to seal one of the boosters.

Three groups of people played central roles in the scenario: the engineers and managers at Thiokol directly responsible for the launch and NASA officials who also approved it. In particular, five people are of interest: Allan McDonald, the project supervisor; Roger Boisjoly, Morton Thiokol's leading expert on booster seals; Robert Lund, the vice president of engineering and an engineer himself; Jerry Mason, his boss; and Larry Mulloy, the manager of the solid rocket booster project for NASA at the Marshall Space Center.

According to testimony to the Rogers Commission, the commission appointed to investigate the disaster, from the very beginning of the development of the rocket boosters, Morton Thiokol engineers working on the rocket boosters had worried about the strength and flexibility of the O-ring sealing mechanism. Using the Titan III O-ring joint sealing mechanism as a model, Thiokol had designed its solid rocket booster with what it thought was a redundant secondary O-ring at each joint to make the shuttle safer. As early as 1977, however, sealing problems led NASA to demand that the joint be redesigned. The joint was not changed, but the O-rings were enlarged. At the same time, the rocket booster itself was streamlined to reduce its weight, making it more vulnerable to joint rotation and thus to sealing difficulties.

As early as the sixth shuttle flight, heat damage to the O-rings was evident, and it became clear in subsequent launches that the secondary O-rings were not redundant because they too suffered erosion. Despite this evidence, the secondary O-rings were reduced in diameter in subsequent design changes, they were thought by some to be redundant, and little was done to change the design of the sealing joint. As early as the seventh launch, Roger Boisjoly sent memos to his superiors at Thiokol warning of the weaknesses of the O-ring configuration. Yet following the seventeenth successful flight, Mulloy described the O-ring erosion as "accepted and indeed expected—and no longer considered an anomaly" (Bell and Esch, 1989, 24; *Report*, 1986, 33).

By early January 1986, Thiokol's engineers determined that the behavior of the rubber O-ring material could not be accurately predicted when atmospheric temperatures were below 30 degrees. In fact, according to Boisjoly, the ideal launch temperature for the O-rings was 50 degrees. On January 27, the day before the scheduled launch, which had been delayed several times, many of the engineers became alarmed, because the weather at Cape Canaveral was particularly cold, and colder weather was predicted for January 28.

Led by McDonald, at least 14 and perhaps as many as 22 engineers in the solid fuel rocket unit, including Boisjoly, formally protested the launch to the vice president of the Wasatch division, Joe Kilminster, who was also senior vice president for space booster programs at Morton Thiokol, and to NASA directly. As manager of the engineering design team, McDonald refused to sign the launch go-ahead release for Thiokol, a signature necessary in order for the launch to proceed. Three concerns were voiced about the launch. First, the engineers were worried that the low temperatures would cause the O-rings to malfunction and the joints to leak. Second, some engineers were concerned that heavy weather would prevent sea recovery of the $40 million dollar boosters that disengage after launch. Third, it was speculated that the predicted ice in the booster support troughs might affect the shuttle orbiter. However, the flexibility of the O-rings had never been tested below 47 degrees. Hence, when asked by Thiokol managers and NASA to provide scientific data that would prove that the O-rings would definitely not seal the joints, the engineers were unable to substantiate their intuitions.

The engineering team at Thiokol reported to Robert Lund, the vice president of engineering. Although under pressure from NASA to override McDonald's refusal, Lund originally would not sign off on the launch, agreeing with his engineers that low temperatures might affect recovery and O-ring performance. However, feeling pressured by NASA's anxiety to launch the *Challenger* and reassured by NASA's confidence in the launch's success, Jerry Mason, to whom Lund reported, told Lund, "[T]ake off [your] engineering hat and put on [your] management hat" (*Report*, 1986, cited in Vaughn, 1996, 318–20). Lund capitulated, agreed to the launch, and Kilminster, senior vice president at Thiokol, signed off for the company.

After the accident both McDonald and Boisjoly reported their prelaunch protests to the Rogers Commission. Almost immediately Morton Thiokol reorganized its Wasatch, Utah, operations where the boosters are designed and made. Morton Thiokol reported that no engineer was fired, demoted, or reassigned. Nevertheless, McDonald, Boisjoly, and other engineers involved in the O-ring project were taken out of direct contact with NASA, a "realignment" that was taken as a demotion by some of the engineers. Kilminster and Lund were reassigned to other divisions of Morton Thiokol, and Mason took early retirement. After the realignment of the engineers, Boisjoly went on "sick leave" and never returned to Thiokol. McDonald took an extended vacation, but as of this writing he is again the manager of the solid booster rocket program and a vice president of Thiokol (Vaughn, 1996; Werhane, 1991b).

In this chapter I outline a basic but sometimes misunderstood assumption. We all perceive, frame, and interact with the world through a conceptual scheme modified by a set of perspectives or mental models. Putting the point metaphorically, we each run our "camera" of the world through certain selective mechanisms: intentions, interests, desires, points of view, or biases, all of which work as selective and restrictive filters. We each have what I call our own metaphysical movies of the world, because they entail projections of one's perspective on the given data of experience. They are analogous to movies, because, like movies, each of our perspectives varies from stark realism to fantasy and even error, and because, like movies, the selective process leaves a great deal of the data of experience "on the cutting room floor." Sometimes some of us have one-track minds. We filter all experience through one point of view, and it is difficult to try to change that perspective. But ordinarily most of us adopt a number of perspectives, depending on the subject matter and our interests, and these perspectives change or can be altered. Ordinarily, too, we can understand the perspectives of another, although one does not always make such an attempt. Socialization, culture, upbringing, education, exposure to art, and, in our culture, the media, one's profession, and one's working milieu all contribute to ways in which we view and deal with the world. Feelings, emotions, and each person's idiosyncratic method for formulating ideas influence, in turn, new perceptions. So our movies are often reinforced by our own continued projection of a certain perspective on whatever we experience.

Sometimes, though, they are influenced, changed, or even radically re-formulated (Werhane, 1991b).

Given that thesis, I suggest that the *Challenger* explosion resulted from differing scripts of the engineers and management at Thiokol and at NASA. In addition, contrasting corporate cultures at Thiokol and its parent, Morton, framed expectations differently. These contrasting scripts, mental models, or "movies" created differing expectations, resulting in conflicting priorities that contributed significantly to the disaster.

CONCEPTUAL SCHEMES

Beginning with Immanuel Kant, philosophers now agree, although not universally, that "our conceptual scheme mediates even our most basic perceptual experiences" (Railton, 1986, 172). We learn from Kant that our minds do not mirror experience or reality. Rather, our minds project and reconstitute experience. His reasoning, in brief, is as follows. Whereas the content of each of our experiences may vary dramatically, the ways in which we organize, order, and think about our experiences are universally the same. For example, Kant argued, we all experience the world in three dimensions, in a space-time continuum, and we engage in similar sorting mechanisms such as quantity, quality, same as, different, equal to, and so forth. Kant also claimed that all humans order the world causally; that is, when an event occurs, we assume it has a cause, and, alternately, all events are assumed to be causally related to other events. Yet we organize our experiences as formal concepts: they lack content and cannot be perceived. For example, one cannot perceive time; one merely experiences events temporally. "Cause" and "effect" are not observable phenomena but ways in which we frame relationships between phenomena. Kant concluded that all human beings order and organize their experiences through an identical set of formal concepts. So, although the content of each of our experiences may be quite different, the ways in which we order these experiences is exactly the same. This would explain how we can imaginatively understand experiences we have never encountered and communicate with people of cultures, ethnic backgrounds, or historical periods quite different from ours.

Do some basic, innate structures of the mind identically order all human experiences, as Kant contended? The subject is controversial. What we glean from Kant is that the mind organizes, orders, and even censors experiences through a conceptual scheme. The idea of a conceptual scheme implies that the notion of reality as "something outside all schemes" (Rorty, 1993, 443) makes no sense.

Somewhat disapprovingly, Donald Davidson describes conceptual

schemes as follows. "Conceptual schemes, we are told, are ways or organizing experience; they are systems of categories that give form to the
data of sensation; they are points of view from which individuals, [in-
stitutions], cultures, or [historical] periods survey the passing scene"
(1974, 5). Davidson's disapproval centers around whether conceptual
schemes are commensurably distinct. If they are not, as he suggests,
then they are philosophically uninteresting. He concludes, "[W]e have
found no intelligible basis on which it can be said that schemes are
different [even though] it would be equally wrong to announce . . .
that all speakers of language, at least, share a common scheme and on-
tology" (1974, 20). Still, the idea of a conceptual scheme helps to examine the notion of differing belief systems or worldviews, because it is not
inconceivable that there are, or have been, more than one belief system
or worldview. But, as I shall argue later in the chapter, conceptual
schemes are not, indeed, cannot be, logically incommensurable. In what
follows I shall distinguish the idea of a conceptual scheme from what scientists and social scientists call mental models, as well as from what
Davidson calls a common coordinate system.

The pervasiveness of conceptual schemes implies that each of us perceives and experiences from a point of view, a perspective that serves as
a selective organizing, filtering, and focusing mechanism. Our conceptual scheme frames our perceptions. It focuses, schematizes, and guides
the ways in which we recognize, react, and organize the world. In fact,
how we define the world is relative to that scheme and thus all reality is
conceptually structured. A conceptual scheme is the means and mode
through which we constitute our experiences, although, I shall argue,
conceptual schemes may not be universally identical. Neither are they,
as Kant thought, all formal concepts of understanding.

Many philosophers argue that conceptual schemes are semantically
based (e.g., Anscombe, 1976; Johnson, 1993; Putnam, 1990; Rorty, 1993;
Wittgenstein, 1953). Whether human beings conceptualize or deal with
the world nonlinguistically is a thesis for another essay, but as Hilary Putnam and Richard Rorty argue, "[E]lements of what we call 'language' or
'mind' *penetrate so deeply into what we call 'reality' that the very project of representing ourselves as being mappers of something 'language-independent' is fatally compromised from the start*" (Putnam, 1990, 28; cited approvingly in
Rorty, 1993, 443; emphasis Rorty's). Language shapes our perspectives
in such deeply grounded ways that it is difficult to imagine how we
would conceptualize or frame experience purely nonlinguistically, because the very act of describing and explaining such concepts and
frames uses language. The question of whether language and linguistic
ability are innate "deep structures," (Chomsky, 1965) hardwired as part
of what it is to be a human being, is also controversial and takes us far
afield from this project. However, all evidence points to three basic facts:

first, no group of human beings has ever been discovered, even in what we might agree are the most primitive situations, that did not have a well-developed, complex spoken language that can generate an almost infinite number of ways of expression in that language. Second, language is socially learned in early childhood. In rare instances children who have been brought up in isolation from other human contact do not speak, and after a certain age, around five, they cannot learn language (Langer, 1942/1951). Third, whereas the fact of language is universal, grammar and syntax vary dramatically, thus framing widely different conceptual schemes that, in turn, create different belief systems.

If languages are the most basic means through which we structure our experiences, they are, in some sense, "metaconceptual schemes" because our language or languages constitute the background framing mechanism for a conceptual scheme. Yet a particular language is often incomplete, because its syntax and grammar can preclude formulation of certain kinds of conceptual schemes. Still, the theoretical possibility of understanding languages whose grammar and syntax are alien to our own (and thus a new conceptual scheme) is not precluded. While specific languages and even dialects are quite different, so that the way they shape and express belief systems is distinct, there is no logically private language that is, in principle, untranslatable. As Ludwig Wittgenstein posited in *Philosophical Investigations,* the notion of a rule-based language assumes a consistency of use so that in principle a language cannot be private; that is, no language is logically and in principle incomprehensible to anyone because rules can be learned (Werhane, 1992; Wittgenstein, 1953). This conclusion does not imply that a word such as "ennui" in French has a one-to-one translation in English. It does not. But it does imply that because the grammar of French follows consistent repeatable patterns that are understandable, I as an English speaker can also learn French. French grammar is different from English grammar, but they both are consistently rule-based constructions that allow a speaker of one language to learn another. It also implies that when I learn French, and enough about French culture, I can understand the meaning of ennui and why it has no exact equivalent in English.

MENTAL MODELS

In *The Fifth Discipline* (1990), Peter Senge explains conceptual schemes in terms of mental models, a term that comes from the cognitive science literature. Although the term is not always clearly defined, mental model connotes the idea that human beings have mental representations, cognitive frames, or mental pictures of their experiences—models of the stimuli or data with which they are interacting—and these are frameworks that set up parameters though which experience, or a certain set of experiences, is organized or filtered (Gentner and Whitley, 1997, 210–1). "Mental models are the mechanisms whereby humans are able to generate descriptions of system purpose and form, explanations of system functioning and observed system states, and predictions of future system states" (Rouse and Morris, 1986, 351). Mental models might be hypothetical constructs of the experience in question or scientific theories; they might be schema that frame the experience, through which individuals process information, conduct experiments, and formulate theories; or mental models may simply refer to human knowledge about a particular set of events or a system. Mental models account for our ability to describe, explain, and predict and may function as protocols to account for human expectations often formulated in accordance with these models (Gorman, 1992, 192–235; Rouse and Morris, 1986).

The notion of a mental model is connected with what Karl Weick and others call sensemaking (Starbuck and Milliken, 1988b; Weick, 1969/1979, 1995). Sensemaking is defined as "placing stimuli into frameworks (or schemata) that make sense of the stimuli" (Starbuck and Milliken, 1988b, 51). This is a process of filtering, categorizing, sorting, framing, extrapolating, and interpreting the stimuli or data. Starbuck and Milliken take a neo-Kantian view that sensemaking, in various forms, is the way we deal with the data of our experiences, as well as the means for understanding, predicting, and explaining human events. Weick uses the term to account for the ways in which we invent, construct, interpret, and even revise our experiences. According to Weick, "[t]he process of sensemaking is intended to include the construction and bracketing of the textlike cues that are interpreted, as well as the revision of those interpretations based on action and its consequences"(Weick, 1995, 8). Sensemaking is an ongoing process of clarification and explanation of situations or events. Thus, according to Weick, sensemaking often occurs retrospectively. That is, we often retrospectively reframe a past event from another point of view in order to clarify or make sense of it. Often this process revises the meaning of the event, reinterprets or even omits data, and reframes its significance (Gioia, 1986; Weick, 1995, 4). For example, in causal examinations of the *Challenger* explosion, moral philosophers tend to frame the event and the processes leading up to the explosion in moral terms, terms that may not have been on the minds of the protagonists at that time. In the case of the *Challenger,* reframing focuses attention on this launch, ignoring the fact that in all the preceding launches there were unpredictable and predictable issues and problems that could have caused an earlier explosion.

According to Paul Churchland, the sensemaking process begins early in small children:

> Children learn to recognize certain prototypical kinds of social situations,
> and they learn to produce or avoid the behaviors prototypically required
> or prohibited in each. Young children learn to recognize a distribution of
> scarce resources such as cookies or candies as a *fair* or *unfair* distribution.
> They learn to voice complaints in the latter case, and to withhold com-
> plaint in the former. (1989, rpt. in Johnson, 1993, 190–1)

I would argue that almost all human activity is sensemaking, in various
forms, and that the operative mechanisms in sensemaking are our use
of mental models. Senge argues that mental models are "deeply held internal images of how the world works, images that limit us to familiar
ways of thinking and acting" (1990, 174). Mental models constitute the
basis for our assumptions and points of view. They are created by theories, myths, stories, and images that frame, focus, or revise the ways we
experience the world.

Examples of mental models and how they function abound. The creation story in the Bible has generated a belief system about the foundation of humanity and reality. Similarly, the Big Bang theory in astron-
omy has framed an explanatory model that shapes the belief system of
those who accept it. Theories about whether human beings are psychological egoists shape our expectations about behavior, about behavioral
control, and about rewards and punishments. If we accept a neoclassical
economic model that we are all, in our rational moments, utility maxi-
mizers, we will think differently about the value of human activities
from, say, those who argue that rationality includes altruism and fairness.

The media, film, art, fiction, myths, and stories, too, shape our mental
models or conceptual schemes. For example, the Marlboro Man adver-
tisements help us to imagine that smoking is masculine and sexy, and
Joe Camel that smoking is "cool." A film such as *Wall Street* can change
not merely our perceptions but our whole point of view about Wall
Street and markets through the model it projects. Mental models, then,
are not merely formal or universal concepts; in fact, their differences
cause us to form parochial points of view and to misunderstand each
other.

A point of view can become indelibly etched in our brain even when it
actually misrepresents experienced phenomena. The art historian E. H.
Gombrich points out the sixteenth-century artist Albrecht Durer's famous woodcut of a rhinoceros depicting the animal with a heavy coat of
armor. This depiction served as a model for renderings of the animal in
natural history books until the eighteenth century, even though, in fact,
for those who are not rhinoceros experts, rhinos do not have armor.
Similarly, an early 1598 engraving depicting a whale with ears served as a
model for whale images, even though whales are earless (Gombrich,
1961, 80–2).

In framing our experiences, mental models also function as focusing projectors. Some aspects of the kinds of projectors we use relate directly to the *Challenger* case. To borrow a phrase from the philosopher Michael Davis, we often have "microscopic vision." That is, we focus on a narrow range of phenomena or data, or we focus on that data in a careful, insightful way. Microscopic vision is crucial in engineering, the sciences, medicine, and other professions for study in great detail (Starbuck and Milliken, 1988a). Roger Boisjoly's focus on O-rings is such an example. He probably knows more about O-rings than anyone else in the field of space technology. But that focused expertise may have interfered with his ability to consider whistleblowing outside the confines of Thiokol on the night before the launch of the *Challenger*, because Boisjoly, according to his own testimony, never considered going around Lund to senior officers at Morton Thiokol or N A S A (Boisjoly, 1988, 17–22). In making that suggestion, I have engaged in retrospective sensemaking, which may or may not accurately fit the event and Boisjoly's thinking at the time. My excuse is to try to make (new) sense out of the event in light of data available at the time of the launch, including the fact that managers and engineers at Thiokol had the home telephone numbers of all the top management at Morton (Hugh Marx, 1986, personal interview).

Let us look again at Dennis Gioia's report of his activities at Ford during the Pinto era to illustrate how mental models can function in specific settings. Gioia had always thought of himself as an extremely moral and socially responsible person. Yet he relates that, while functioning as recall coordinator, he was exposed to reports of Pintos "lighting up," "cars simply . . . consumed by fire after apparently very low speed accidents" (Gioia, 1992, 381). Some of the few actual reports of Pinto explosions contained detailed photographs including, in at least one incident, a report and photos of a number of people who were killed by the fire. After viewing one actual burned-out Pinto, Gioia brought up the Pinto model for departmental review as a possible recall. But after considering the case, neither Gioia nor anyone else at that meeting recommended recalling the model. Gioia was convinced by his own reasoning process and by other seemingly thoughtful managers not to recall those cars because, the managers argued, the evidence was not conclusive that the Pinto was more defective than its competitors, many subcompact autos had been subject to similar dreadful accidents, and the Pinto was a popular, best-selling auto.

Gioia left Ford in 1975 to work on a PhD. Later, when asked by his students why he did not order a recall, Gioia reports how he had learned to view his job through a "Ford-trained" perspective:

> On moral grounds I knew I could recommend most of the vehicles on my safety tracking record for recall (and risk earning the label of a "bleeding heart"). On practical grounds, I recognized that people implicitly accept

risks in cars. We could not recall all cars with *potential* problems and stay in business. I learned to be responsive to those cases that suggested an imminent, dangerous problem. (1992, 382)

Looking back on this scenario Gioia concludes:

My own schematized (scripted) knowledge influenced me to perceive recall issues in terms of the prevailing decision environment and to unconsciously overlook key features of the Pinto case, mainly because they did not fit an existing script. Although the outcomes of the [Pinto] case carry retrospectively obvious ethical overtones, the schemas driving my perceptions and actions precluded consideration of the issues in ethical terms because the scripts did not include ethical dimensions. (1992, 385)

While at Ford, Gioia did not step out of his role as recall coordinator and, as a manager at Ford, explore the ramifications of this situation. He did not translate common-sense personal moral principles into his perception of his professional responsibilities, leaving a gap between his personal morality and his performance as recall coordinator. The corporate culture at Ford reinforced this division by not framing issues in terms that would raise questions about the viability of continuing to sell a defective automobile. At the time, Gioia was not aware of the gap between his personal moral beliefs and his professional behavior, he had little realization that there was a distinctive "Ford perspective," and he did not imagine that this perspective was just that—one of a number of possible ways to deal with burned-up Pintos. It was only later, in retrospection, that Gioia became conscious of the thinking processes or "scripts" active in his belief system while he was engaged at Ford.

Gioia defines a mental model, or what he calls a schema, as "a cognitive framework that people use to impose structure upon information, situations, and expectations to facilitate understanding (1992, 385). Gioia distinguishes schemas from scripts: "A *script* is a specialized type of schema that retains knowledge of actions appropriate for specific situations and contexts. . . . [S]cripts . . . provide a cognitive framework for *understanding* information and events as well as a guide to appropriate *behavior* to deal with the situation faced" (1992, 385). Mental models, then, can function as specific framing scripts or mini belief systems in specific kinds of situations or within the culture of institutions such as corporations.

Because of the pervasiveness of mental models, "as human beings we cannot have a view of the world that does not reflect our interests and values" (Putnam, 1990, 178; Rorty, 1993, 443). One way we deal with experience is normatively, through such notions as what ought one to do, what is right or wrong, what is good or bad, useful or destructive, and so on. Moral theories, such as utilitarianism or deontology, give us prototypical mental models with which to deal with these notions. Moral theories are mental models, systemic ways or models for thinking about normative issues, which themselves are schematized. So when one applies an ethical theory (or theories) to a set of incidents such as Ford's manufacture of the Pinto, or Thiokol's design of O-rings, one is layering another interpretation or schema on an already schematized situation. No wonder, then, that sometimes moral theories fail to trigger new thinking or decision-making by their proponents.

Not all mental models are cognitive. According to a number of contemporary philosophers and psychologists, another form of social construction is our emotions. A great deal of evidence suggests that our emotions, like our belief structures, are not merely innate, inchoate, brute outbursts. Rather, they, too, are socially constructed and learned. One learns both what emotions are and how to feel just as one learns what is good or evil, true or false, red or green, and the meaning of emotions varies culturally just as language does (Harre, 1986; Nussbaum, 1990, 287–94; Rorty, 1980). So, for example, ancient Greek color words are not easily translatable because their emotional meanings are quite different from ours. To illustrate, consider that Euripides describes blood as "green" or "yellow green." From a contemporary English-speaking point of view, this is a curious expression. However, for the ancient Greeks green was associated with youth or fear. In that context "green blood" makes sense (Dancy, 1983; Irwin, 1974).

Our own idiosyncratic interests, feelings, desires, and points of view also affect our mental models. Each of us perceives and deals with experience through perspectives that include our interests, desires, points of view, or biases, as well as cognitive and emotional frames through which we selectively frame and filter experience. Each of us has, or is capable of having, a number of overlapping schema that may function differently in different contexts. These mental models do not merely frame our experiences; indeed, they function as selective mechanisms and filters for dealing with experience. We also "color" our experiences through our passions, feelings, intentions, interests, and foci, so that we each have an idiosyncratic way of shaping our experiences. In selecting, focusing, framing, organizing, and ordering what we experience, conceptual schemes bracket and leave out data, and emotional and motivational foci taint or color experience. Nevertheless, because schema we employ are socially learned and altered through religion, socialization, culture, educational upbringing, and other experiences, they are shared ways of perceiving and organizing experience; through our common language we can understand and communicate conceptual differences of each of our mental models.

HOW MENTAL MODELS ARE LIMITING

Because of the variety and diversity of mental models, none is complete, and "there are multiple possible framings of any given situation" (Johnson, 1993, 9). By that I mean that each of us can frame any situation,

event, or phenomenon in more that one way, and that same phenomenon can also be socially constructed in a variety of ways. The way one
frames a situation is critical to its outcome, because "[t]here are . . .
different moral consequences depending on the way we frame the situation" (Johnson, 1993, 9). This, as we saw, is clearly exemplified in Gioia's
depiction of his thought processes as recall coordinator at Ford compared to his retrospective analysis of his activities.

In the *Challenger* case the ways in which different parties framed risk
measurements resulted in radically different perceptions of the dangers
of the space shuttles. Richard Feynman, a Nobel Prize physicist and
member of the Rogers Commission, is most famous for placing an O-
ring in a glass of ice water at one of the Rogers Commission hearings.
The O-ring cracked in the ice water, thus allegedly proving the contention that the weather was too cold to launch on January 28. While
serving on the commission, Feynman interviewed a number of NASA officials, engineers, and managers after the *Challenger* explosion. Feynman
found that estimates of the probability of booster failure ranged from as
high as 1 in 10 to as low as 1 in 100,000. According to Feynman, NASA
engineers at Huntsville placed the probability of failure at 1 in 300, the
rocket designers and builders at 1 in 10,000, an independent consulting
firm claimed at 1 or 2 in 100, and NASA installers at the Kennedy
launch pad at 1 in 100,000. Hence, each professional dealt with the
same or similar data differently. These conflicting analyses resulted in
part from different perceptions of how to interpret the predictability of
the statistics and from different belief systems operative in NASA,
Thiokol, and the thinking of the various NASA contractors (Feynman,
1989). Feynman and others conjecture that while a failure would have
made NASA and Thiokol more vigilant and creative in seeking new systems that would not fail again, success bred complacency. This aura of
confidence became the dominating script at Thiokol and NASA. The
failures and flaws during the many flights that preceded the *Challenger*
were interpreted as "normal." In fact, according to some analyses, success implied a higher probability of future successes, so that eventually,
at NASA at least, some managers projected a very slight likelihood of
failure—1 in 100,000! Each successful launch was interpreted as reducing the risk of failure for the next launch, and after 24 launches the projected likelihood of failure became minimal (Starbuck and Milliken,
1988b, 319–40).

A second illustration of conflicting frameworks for risk measurement
is exemplified by the confusion on the night before the launch when
the engineers were asked to prove that the O-rings would fail at temperatures below 50 degrees. From their point of view, this was the wrong
question to ask. Engineers usually interpret lack of proof that something will fail as evidence of greater risk. In this case, at least, the man-

agers interpreted the inability of the engineers to prove on short notice that the O-rings would fail in low temperatures as an increased likelihood of success. So, while the engineers could not answer the question about O-ring failure from a managerial perspective, others misinterpreted their silence as reason for hope. The engineers did not adequately comprehend the managerial interpretation of risk, and managers, in turn, did not take seriously the negative relationship between the paucity of test data and O-ring performance at low temperatures. Each group had a different metaphysical movie, and neither realized that they were not communicating.

This also explains Lund's readiness to put on his "managerial hat." Lund had virtually quit the engineering movie—he understood the managerial perspective, but microscopically—without considering any longer an engineering perspective about risk. Lund simply changed frameworks without understanding what he was doing. According to Davis (1989), Lund considered the risk of on-time performance, keeping one's contract, and public relations, concerns not always in the forefront of engineering calculus. Lund balanced that risk against benefits, whereas an engineer might have balanced risks against risks. One could contend that Lund's decision was the best one from his perspective as a manager, considering his analysis of the statistical probability of success. But if managers in Lund's position are supposed to take into account overall conditions, facts, and likely outcomes, Lund failed (Messick and Bazerman, 1996; Werhane, 1991b).

As I pointed out in chapter 2, the engineers at Thiokol likely saw themselves as engineers who make recommendations, not managerial decisions. This partially explains their acceptance of the decision and the fact that they did not "blow the whistle" before the launch, despite their reservations. For surely, just as we asked why Lund accepted NASA's pressures, we should ask, too, why no engineer "went around" management at Thiokol to the CEO of Morton, to the head of NASA, or to the media to question the launch decision before the fact. We see, then, each set of actors running a movie on their own projectors, evidence of strong role identification both on the part of the engineers and Lund as manager, and indeed, perhaps, some "engineering license" with interpretation of the data from O-ring failure in previous launches—attaching armor on rhinos.

There is a third limiting mental model in this scenario—the corporate cultures in which the *Challenger* was developed, the culture of Thiokol and Morton. Morton, the parent company of Morton Thiokol, until its recent divestment of Thiokol, was originally a salt company, but recent mergers with other companies have diversified its portfolio. Nevertheless, the same human resource management policies are in place supposedly for its divisions and subsidiaries. The parent company perceives itself as having an open door employee policy. The company directory publishes the home telephone numbers of all its management, and it is not uncommon for the vice president of human resources or even the CEO to receive calls or visits from personnel at all levels of the company with employee complaints. While a grievance procedure is not in place for all employees, the company tries to deal with each personnel problem individually and sensitively, and the hierarchical organizational chart is not thought to create a barrier for employee contact with top management (Marx, 1986).

The corporate culture at Thiokol was different, not substantially altered after the takeover by Morton. Thiokol had been run by 10 managers, nine of whom left Thiokol with substantial golden parachutes when Morton acquired that company. According to a number of commentators, the employment relationship at Thiokol was rigidly hierarchic. This in itself is not necessarily bad. But such a rigid hierarchy often greatly hinders communication between different levels of management and, in this case, between managers and engineers. The Wasatch division, particularly, was administered autocratically; employee complaints were discouraged, and no one thought to "end run" a boss to protest some action or policy.

The corporate culture at the Wasatch division very likely played a crucial role in creating a script that virtually prevented prelaunch whistleblowing. The old Thiokol culture demanded unquestioned loyalty from engineers such as McDonald and Boisjoly. According to Boisjoly, because the managers and the engineers may not have communicated with each other adequately, they did not either read the data properly or pay due attention to Boisjoly's early warning admonitions about the O-ring design (1988, 17–22). There was lack of communication and likely an absence of trust between managers and engineers, thus a subsequent isolation of managers from proper reading of the data. So it is not surprising that the engineers involved in the rocket booster program did not imagine they could make an appeal beyond their divisional managers, even in a crisis situation such as the *Challenger* launch, despite the availability by telephone of the CEO and other top managers at Morton.

Morton Thiokol, the parent company, had a responsibility in this merger, in line with its policies and culture, to examine the cultural situation of its Wasatch operations, to change the script operating at Thiokol so that avenues for whistle-blowing could be opened up. Yet it is insufficient to conclude that Morton was simply negligent. Morton is perceived as a well-managed company with thoughtful senior officers and a strong middle management. I would like to suggest that something different was at work here—another kind of mental model of corporate mergers (Werhane, 1988, 1990b). Morton bought Thiokol, a profitable underpriced company, because Morton had a surplus of cash after divesting itself of a pharmaceutical company (Norwich) and because Thiokol had a profitable chemical division. Thiokol was an investment, not the purchase of a company whose products and goals matched Morton's interests or synergy. But Morton had to buy the rocket booster division of Thiokol in order to acquire the chemical companies.

Morton's thinking of Thiokol as an investment may have led to neglect of many Thiokol stakeholders. Reputation suggests that although Morton, the parent, is an ethically conscientious company, it failed to consider that it had the same level of moral responsibility to its subsidiary, Thiokol, as well as responsibility for the behavior of Thiokol. Perhaps the culture of that subsidiary and its stakeholder relationships simply did not come under consideration or at least was not internalized as part of Morton's mission. If this was not the case, it is difficult to explain its thoughtless approach to Thiokol and its divestment after the explosion of the rocket booster division of Thiokol (but it kept the chemical companies). What was missing in Morton was the moral imagination to examine the "inside" of its acquisition of Thiokol, to see how that corporate culture differed from Morton's, and how such differences might make a difference. As a result, Thiokol engineers worked within the old hierarchical structure at Thiokol without adequate information about their new opportunities to speak out.

The other organization deeply involved in the shuttle launch was NASA. A careful study of that organization would require another chapter. But briefly, one cannot help but wonder how it conceptualized its data analysis and conclusions about the probabilities of a launch failure. Although it is usually argued that NASA was under pressure from the president and the media to launch the shuttle, according to the Rogers Commission report, the NASA managers themselves contended they did not internalize this pressure as a decisive influence in their decision to launch. Rather, apparently they were confident that this shuttle launch, like the others, would not fail. Mulloy, a middle manager at NASA and the NASA person closest to the O-ring situation, made the final decision to launch without even communicating to his superiors Thiokol's objections to launch. According to Mulloy, there were no criteria that took into account low temperatures, no "rule" (mental model) by which to raise that question, so he approved its going ahead (*Report,* 1986). Perhaps, as Howard Schwartz has suggested, Mulloy, like others working on this project, was so impressed with NASA's previous successes that he could not imagine O-ring failure, despite contrary evidence from many previous launches (Schwartz, 1987, 1988).

Like the engineers and managers at Thiokol, NASA managers failed to examine their agency and its mission from any perspective except their own. Taking another perspective is crucial, because unless one can disengage oneself from the context of specific decisions, from one's particular "movie," decisions become parochially embedded and result in business decisions that threaten public safety and thus invite moral and fiscal failure. International or not, these decisions set precedents, and others follow those precedents. Optimism at NASA after each launch set a precedent for the next launch, a precedent that encouraged a relaxation of engineering caution. This NASA point of view created models for other similar actions and set precedents difficult to resist or reverse. According to Feynman, "They fooled themselves" (*Report*, 1986, 156).

The *Challenger* disaster clearly illustrates the limiting nature of mental models. A certain mental model develops or is adopted that frames the scenario in which one is operating so that often we fail to see the limitations and finite perspectives, even distortions, of our worldview. A mental model is just that—a model—one of several ways to frame a situation with a number of other possibilities. When we fail to recognize these limitations, the consequences are sometimes worse than painted ears on whales.

INCOMMENSURABILITY AND THE ALLEGED RELATIVISM OF CONCEPTUAL SCHEMES

Because "the very project of representing ourselves as being mappers of something 'language-independent' is fatally compromised," as Putnam and Rorty assent, it is sometimes argued that conceptual schemes are incommensurable with one another so that one cannot "translate" one scheme to another or understand the concepts embedded in a scheme other than one's own.[2] (Gioia and Pitré, 1991; Jackson and Carter, 1991). Some writers argue that the issue is whether conceptual schemes (i.e., belief systems or worldviews) are incommensurable with each other (e.g., Davidson, 1974; Kuhn, 1962/1970). Other writers such as Gioia and Pitré—in an early paper that Gioia later questions in his work with Gary Weaver (Weaver and Gioia, 1994)—appear to be introducing the notion of incommensurability to apply, in a more restricted sense, to mental models or what Gioia calls schema. Although the distinction is blurry, the term "mental model" usually refers to incomplete, learned, and revisable schema. If such schema are *individually* incommensurable, then one is left with the problem of solipsism. If these schemas are institutionally, socially, culturally, or parochially theory-based, so as to be logically incommensurable with other mental models, one faces an issue Donald Davidson calls conceptual relativism. According to Davidson, conceptual relativism is the thesis that

> [t]here may be no translating from one to another, in which case the beliefs, desires, hopes, and bits of knowledge that characterize one person

have no true counterparts for the subscribed to another scheme. Reality itself is relative to a scheme; what counts as real in one system may not in another. (1974, 5)

Although Davidson is referring to conceptual schemes in this quotation, if mental models are incommensurable with each other, his conclusions apply to mental models as well. The question of solipsism is interesting, but I do not address it in this book, because in chapter 2 I argued that human beings are intrinsically social: we survive, develop, and mature only in a social context with other beings like ourselves. Earlier in this chapter, I argued that a private language, that, by its structure, is incomprehensible to anyone other than its speaker, is impossible. If both these theses are correct, if a mental model is socially inculcated through language and through other cultural media, and if mental models are incomplete, then they are shared or shareable with others. So idiosyncratic differences in how each of us deals with experience, and differences between cultures, languages, historical periods, and religions can, at least in theory, be comprehended and understood, although certainly not always shared or agreed upon.

Conceptual relativism, in referring strictly to conceptual schemes, is a stickier issue. This type of relativism argues that certain worldviews or "constellation[s] of beliefs, values, techniques, and scientific structures" (Kuhn, 1962/1970, 175) are incommensurable with each other; the views are mutually exclusive or conflict on such basic grounds that one cannot hold any two such views simultaneously. One could argue further that some worldviews are strongly or "dramatically" incommensurable, that is, incomprehensible to one another so that someone who functions within worldview A could not comprehend worldview B or communicate with those who held it. It would follow from this second form of incommensurability that reasoning (and thus moral reasoning) would be solely scheme-dependent and that one's reasoning processes simply could not function as *reasoning* in a worldview incommensurable with one's own.

These two forms of conceptual relativism reach quite different conclusions. The first formulation claims that some worldviews are incommensurable with each other—so that one could not advocate both simultaneously without contradiction—illustrated by, say, the Ptolemaic versus the Copernican view of the universe. It is obviously impossible to hold both that the world is the center of the universe and that it is not, and theory and data interpretations that support each view by and large contradict each other. One cannot simultaneously be thoroughly Ptolemaic and thoroughly Copernican. Nevertheless, one can *understand* both views and their theoretical baggage, and Ptolemains can communicate meaningfully with Copernicans; that is, these theories are not strongly incommensurable. To change from a Ptolemaic to a Copernican view, one must change many of the mental models operative in one's worldview, if not the entire concepual scheme. Still, there is a basic mode of communication underlying both views that remains unaffected by this paradigm shift and accounts for the fact that we can recognize, acknowledge, and label that shift. According to Davidson, "[d]ifferent points of view make sense but only if there is a common coordinate system on which to plot them; that the existence of a common system belies the claim of dramatic incomparability" (1974, 6). Thus, paradigm differences between conceptual schemes do not necessarily imply strong incommensurability.

What is meant by a "common coordinate system"? Wittgenstein, Rorty, Davidson, and Putnam all claim, in different ways, that the common system is semantics or the fact of language (Davidson, 1974; Putnam, 1990; Rorty, 1993; Wittgenstein, 1953). What is important for our purposes is the distinction between a common coordinate system and conceptual schemes. Social practices, histories, or rule-following activities including particular languages, are mental models, part of one's conceptual scheme, and neither system nor scheme is logically private or incomprehensible to each other. The common coordinate system we share as human beings is a precondition for human activities that include language; it is the "bedrock" for a variety of languages and other conceptual schemes. The distinction between conceptual scheme and common coordinate system reveals how we share common perspectives and how we can understand the language and the perspectives, of historically or culturally distant people. Indeed, a conceptual scheme and the possibility of both being aware of a conceptual scheme and revising it makes sense only if we assume a common coordinate system that precludes strong incommensurability or what Davidson calls "dramatic incommensurability."[3]

Dramatic or strong incommensurability, the view that two conceptual schemes or worldviews might be incomprehensible in principle to one another, such that a person operating within one belief system could not comprehend the belief system of a second, implies that certain languages, institutions, cultures, or scientific theses can be logically private on a macro level because they are incomprehensible to anyone other than their speaker, adherents, and believers. According to this thesis, languages, cultures, or schemes would exhibit ways of identifying, connecting, iterating, and repeating in patterns with a kind of consistency unknown to the rest of us. That is, there would be different common coordinate systems; indeed, terms like "common," "coordinate," and "system" would have unrecognizable meanings. The connections and patterns of reidentification would be utterly different from the ways we understand these terms, so different that we could not conceive of how such a constellation of conceptual schemes could operate as a belief *system*.

It is nearly impossible to imagine another possible worldview that does not exhibit some characteristics of consistency, repeatability, or identity, some rule-based characteristics that would bind it together as a worldview. Yet dramatic incommensurability demands that notions such as consistency, rule-following, identity or sameness would be utterly different in two conceptual schemes. This difference would bar our comprehension of the other worldview. Thus, what dramatic incommensurability seems oxymoronic.

There is still a third way to think of conceptual relativism, in particular the thesis that because we cannot view experience from "nowhere," that is, from a position that is not tainted by language or some mental model, "[r]eality itself is relative to a scheme; what counts as real in one system may not in another" (Davidson, 1974, 5). If all our experience is shaped by a conceptual scheme, then what we mean by "reality," or the "world," or even "experience" is similarly shaped by a conceptual scheme, so what might be perceived as "real" in one scheme would not be so perceived in another. The result would be a form of linguistic idealism, the idea that "essence is *created* by grammar" (Anscombe, 1976, 188).

There is one sense in which this thesis is plausible. What counts as "fact" for example, is different for different peoples, depending on whether and how their particular belief system treats myth, story, and scientifically verifiable data. These differences in what is fact or "true" can be seen even within a particular societal belief system. For example, in the United States we might assume that everyone, or at least every reasonable adult, has adapted a belief system that accepts as true what scientists have called verifiable facts. However, to look at one instance, in the Dow Corning Company (DCC) breast implant controversies (see more discussion in the next chapter), the scientific epidemiological evidence overwhelmingly posits a very weak correlation at best between breast implants and any known disease (Angell, 1996; Brinton and Brown, 1997). Yet 440,000 women with implants have joined in a class action suit against DCC, claiming they are ill as a result of their breast implants. Most of these women are truly ill with something, and juries have awarded large settlements against DCC to ill women with implants, often citing the fact of the illnesses to back up their judgments that these illnesses were caused by implants. Perhaps the jurors have simply conflated the fact of illnesses with the existence of implants in the ill women. But because that sort of judgment belies what scientists would call a ground for "good evidence," another phenomenon is at work in these instances: the fact of the illnesses and their emotional connection to implants. Thus, notions of truth and factual evidence are not consistent even among intelligent Americans.

Nevertheless, there is a difference between claiming that one cannot get at reality, or the world, or experience except through some conceptual scheme, and concluding that reality or experience is itself *merely* created or *solely* socially constructed. Arguing that the incomplete, disparate ways in which we present and distill experience are socially constructed is different from arguing that experience or reality *itself* is socially created. I argue here that how we conceive the world is conceptually dependent, that is, "[e]ssence is *expressed* by grammar" (Wittgenstein, 1953, § 371, my italics). This is quite different from concluding that "essence is created by grammar." When essence is *created* by grammar, we call it lying, fantasy, storytelling, or mythmaking. Within any belief system we are careful to distinguish fantasy and myth from "the real," "the true," or "the facts," even though each is socially structured. In the DCC breast implant controversies, we are still looking for ways to account for the fact that 440,000 women with implants claim to be ill and to correlate that set of claims with the contrasting epidemiological data.

CONCLUSION

The *Challenger* disaster demands that we examine carefully not just the case but also our perspectives and our biases. It invites us to question our habits and models of dealing with the world, to look into ourselves to find out how we make choices, and sometimes to question our presuppositions. Scientists and engineers, in particular, who work with allegedly "hard" data, are often misled into thinking that data is purely objective, forgetting that such data has usually been filtered through constructs such as a particular scientific model. Seldom do we heed what Werner Heisenberg (1932, 1959) taught us some 60 years ago, that even the most allegedly unbiased observations of an event affect that event. One needs to develop more critically evaluative perspectives even in engineering and scientific analyses and most surely in the use of statistics. Otherwise, we live in a costly twilight zone of our own mental models dictated by job-related roles, institutional mores, or ingrained habits.

Given that all are activities are embedded in a conceptual scheme and framed by mental models, are such critically evaluative perspectives possible? I think so; I have just been engaged in an examination of a number of perspectives and their limitations. Because no conceptual schemes are logically incommensurable, and because mental models are incomplete and alterable, we can perceive conceptual schemes, find out which mental models are operative, to change our modes of intention, projection, and perception, and even modify our definitions of "fact" and "fantasy" without succumbing to the conclusion that all our experiences are mere storytelling. Part of the activity of critical thinking is traceable to the thin aspect of the self I discussed in chapter 2. The self is more than its thick social interconnections and relationships, and in its evaluative, critical mode it perceives different perspectives and questions some of its roles, relationships, and previous decisions. As I claim in chapter 5, one may not ever achieve a totally objective point of view. One can never examine oneself or one's experiences divorced from any context or frame. On the other hand, since each mental model is only a partial perspective, one can often analyze the mental models at work, the "movies" playing, and the schemas that affect and even limit decision-making from a critical perspective of the thin or core self.

This process of engaging in a critical perspective on oneself, one's activities, one's behavior, and one's situation is what I call the development of moral imagination, which I treat in detail in chapter 5. It involves, at a minimum, asking difficult questions and attempting to place oneself in a different perspective so as to regard events from another point of view, individual, organizational, and social. There is no guarantee that one will always achieve a sufficient distance from a particular dilemma or derive the best decision because distancing oneself may also lead to *moral* distancing so that the moral implications of the dilemma are bracketed as well. Still, as I assert in chapter 6, a process of questioning and a critically distancing oneself to test one's decisions can be steps toward a more engaged moral decision-making process and, more important, to moral responsibility. This sort of approach was not taken by the engineers, managers, or NASA officials involved in the *Challenger* incident. This sort of stance is what philosophers call a supererogatory act, an act that requires courage and leadership, the kind of leadership we seldom see. Of course, there is always the possibility that if Lund, Thiokol's engineers, or Mulloy had raised any of these issues with the top management at NASA or at Morton headquarters, these managers might have decided to launch the *Challenger* anyway. Moreover, such actions do not always turn out well, as evidenced by the history of whistle-blowers, most of whom have been fired, blackballed from their industry or profession, and suffered personal problems. But maybe, just possibly, top managers at Morton or at NASA would have taken a risk, a moral risk, and stopped the launch process. Interestingly, after the disaster the chief engineer at Thiokol and leader of the protesting engineers before the launch, Allan McDonald, was promoted at Thiokol. This is one of the few counterinstances when a whistle-blower has been reinstated and promoted to an even more responsible position. The bottom line is that each individual and each corporation is responsible, morally responsible, when they have requisite knowledge and the ability and possibility to choose. Developing the requisite moral imagination and moral leadership is crucial if disasters such as the *Challenger* are to be avoided. Morton Thiokol demonstrated an inkling of that imagination after *Challenger*. In chapters 5 and 6 I examine moral imagination further to see how this might be possible.

> I can't characterize it as an "accident" at all. It was a horrible, terrible disaster. But not an accident. Because we could have stopped it. We had initially stopped it. And then the decision was made to go forward anyways.
> Roger Boisjoly (Maier, 1992/1994, 26)

4

The *Rashomon* Effect

The Academy Award–winning 1950 Japanese movie *Rashomon* depicts an incident involving an outlaw, a rape or seduction of a woman, and a murder or suicide of her husband. A passerby, who is also the narrator, explains how the story is told to officials from four different perspectives: that of the outlaw, the woman, the husband, and himself. The four narratives agree that the outlaw, wandering through the forest, came upon the woman on a horse led by her husband; the outlaw tied up the husband; the woman and the outlaw had intercourse in front of the bound husband; and the husband was found dead. The narratives do not agree on how these events occurred or who killed the husband. The outlaw contends that consensual intercourse occurred between him and the wife, and he claims to have killed the husband. The wife depicts the sexual act as rape and claims that because of her disgrace, she killed her husband. The husband, through a medium, says that the sexual act began as rape and ended as consent, and that, in shame after being untied by the outlaw, he killed himself. The passerby's story confirms the husband's account of the sexual contact but claims that the bandit was initially afraid to kill the husband. The passerby depicted both men as cowards, preferring to save their own lives rather than protect the wife. Eventually, however, the husband was killed by the bandit. Interestingly, because the passerby is also the narrator of the film, recounting to friends the strange contradictory reportings of this event, we tend to believe his version. But what actually took place is never resolved.

In the preceding chapters I used a series of cases or narratives that depicted incidents in corporate decision-making. In this chapter I

69

examine the role of narratives and make the following claim: the ways we present or re-present a story, the narrative we employ, and the conceptual framing of that story affect its content, its moral analysis, and the subsequent evaluation (Chambers, 1996, 25). Sometimes, narratives of a particular set of events contradict each other. Other times, when one narrative becomes dominant, we appeal to that story for reinforcement of facts, assuming it represents what actually happened, even though it may have distorting effects. The result in either case is a *Rashomon* effect. Yet we seldom carefully examine the narrative we use, often unaware of the "frame" or mental model at work. If my thesis is correct, it is important, morally important, to understand the constructive nature and limits of narratives.

In chapter 3 I argued that all experience is framed and interpreted through a conceptual scheme and a set of mental models that function on the individual, institutional, societal, and cross-cultural levels. We can neither experience nor present a story except through a mental model. Depending on which models are operative, interpretations of a situation or event by persons, groups, institutions, or societies may differ greatly. In chapter 2 I argued that without social relationships, and undefined by social roles, we are, at best, amorphous, ill-defined subjects. Nevertheless, I argued further, we are not merely the sum of, or identified with, these relationships and roles; we can evaluate and change our relationships, roles, and role obligations; and we are thus responsible for them. So, too, we can also create, evaluate, and change our mental models, although the process ordinarily demands a highly developed moral imagination, as I explain in chapter 5.

I now want to add another dimension to the idea of a conceptual scheme and mental models. If humans are intrinsically social beings, who we are and how we develop depend on a network of cultural and social relationships into which we are born and grow up. As a number of philosophers have argued, we are born into and depend on a world that is historically situated; linguistically, socially, and culturally defined; and usually in some process of evolution or change. We are born in the middle of a particular set of historical, political, economic, and social narratives or stories that we neither created nor chose. These narratives define our early roles, as children, as women or men, as tribal members, as worshippers, as citizens (MacIntyre, 1981, 199, 201; Sartre, 1956). These narratives and the language in which they are embedded are the background for individual experiences. They provide the initial conditions for the conceptual schemes we adapt that frame all our experiences, and they often direct, influence, or confine the range of mental models we learn and adapt. Nevertheless, if Davidson is correct, background narratives themselves function as revisable conceptual schemes that are neither static nor incommensurable with each other. Thus, none of us is identified with our socially constructed thick selves; neither are we merely determined by our background historical/social narratives. We are at once byproducts of, characters in, and authors of, our own stories (e.g., Johnson, 1993, 153; Sartre, 1956). Still, sometimes we become so embroiled in a particular set of narratives, of our own making or not, that we fail to compare it with other accounts or evaluate its implications.

In addition to background narratives, our reports of events are also in narrative form:

> All stories are shaped by a particular teller for a particular purpose, for all narratives are infected by their situatedness. Consequently [any story], even though it may be based on a real life event, is mediated and thereby interpreted through narrative discourse . . . and a point of view adopted. (Chambers, 1996, 25)

Sometimes these allegedly true stories, these narrative accounts of actual events, take on a life of their own, one narrative becomes dominant, and we look to that account for data about the event without questioning its perspective or the basis for its "facts." In other instances we find two or more contradictory narratives functioning side by side in the same milieu. In still other cases, narratives of the event in question become explanatory stories without any independent data to support their claims.

To demonstrate, I will recount different narratives of a series of cases: Ford Pinto, the DCC breast implant controversies, and the Salomon Brothers Treasury bond trading episodes. Each of these sets of narratives illustrates different forms of a *Rashomon* effect at work. The Pinto cases demonstrate how one narrative of the Pinto accidents dominated, afterward confused with, and substituted for, other, more reliable accounts. Stories of the DCC controversies illustrate how at least two contradictory narratives could be accepted at the same time. Analyses of the Salomon Brothers Treasury bond episodes illustrate how narratives we create can become coherent, self-referential models that take on the role of explanatory truth, even without any evidence that they represent actual events or the intentions of the protagonists in the narrative. Each set of narratives illustrates, in different ways, that narratives can confuse, bias, and even create what we take to be data, or facts, or even truth.

THE PINTO CASES

Let us begin with some accounts of the Ford Pinto. The accounts of these cases are Mark Dowie's "Pinto Madness" from *Mother Jones,* later revised and reprinted in *Business and Society;* "Beyond Products Liability" by Michael Schmitt and William W. May from the *University of Detroit*

Journal of Urban Law; Manuel Velasquez's treatment of the Pinto in his book *Business Ethics* (second edition); Dekkers L. Davidson and Kenneth Goodpaster's Harvard Business School case, "Managing Product Safety: The Ford Pinto"; Ford Motor Company's statements from its lawsuit, *State of Indiana vs. Ford Motor Company;* and Michael Hoffman's case/essay, "The Ford Pinto." Reporting on these incidents, different commentators present "independently supportable facts" (Schmitt and May, 1979, 1022). In each instance, the commentator claims to be presenting facts, not assumptions, commentary, or conjecture. Yet these "facts" seem to differ. One report, Mark Dowie's, one of the earliest accounts of the case, becomes the dominant narrative despite some of its suspect claims.

The Grimshaw/Pinto case began the documentation of a series of Pinto automobile fires involving rear-end collisions, usually at low speeds, that caused the gas tanks in the Pintos to explode. There is *one* indisputable set of data upon which all commentators agree:

> On May 28, 1972 Mrs. Lily Gray was driving a six-month old Pinto on Interstate 15 near San Bernardino, California. In the car with her was Richard Grimshaw, a thirteen-year old boy. . . . Mrs. Gray stopped in San Bernardino for gasoline, got back onto the freeway (Interstate 15) and proceeded toward her destination at sixty to sixty-five miles per hour. As she approached Route 30 off-ramp, . . . the Pinto suddenly stalled and coasted to a halt in the middle lane. . . . [T]he driver of a 1962 Ford Galaxie was unable to avoid colliding with the Pinto. Before impact the Galaxie had been braked to a speed of from twenty-eight to thirty-seven miles per hour.
>
> At the moment of impact, the Pinto caught fire and its interior burst into flames. The crash had driven the Pinto's gas tank forward and punctured it against the flange on the differential housing. . . . Mrs. Gray died a few days later. . . . Grimshaw managed to survive with severe burns over 90 per cent of his body. (*Grimshaw v. Ford Motor Co.,* 1978, 359; Velasquez, 1988, 122)

What is the background behind the development of the Pinto? Lee Iacocca, then CEO of Ford, stated publicly that in order to meet Japanese competition, Ford decided to design a subcompact car that would weigh less than 2,000 pounds and cost less than $2,000 (Davidson and Goodpaster, 1983). According to Davidson and Goodpaster, Ford began planning the Pinto in June 1967 and began producing it in September 1970. This represented a 38-month turn-around time as opposed to the industry average of 43 months for engineering and developing a new automobile (Davidson and Goodpaster, 1983, 4). Mark Dowie claims that the development was "rushed" into 25 months (1977a, 20); Velasquez says it occurred in "under two years" (1988, 120); Hoffman claims that Ford "rushed the Pinto into production in much less than the usual time" (1984, 133). Although the actual time of development may seem unimportant, critics of the Pinto design argue that *because* it was "rushed into production," the Pinto was not as carefully designed or as carefully checked for safety as a model created over a 43-month time span (Dowie, 1977a; Velasquez, 1988). But if it took 38 months rather than 25, perhaps the Pinto was not rushed into production after all.

The Pinto was designed so that the gas tank was placed behind the rear axle. According to Davidson and Goodpaster, "[a]t that time almost every American-made car had the fuel tank located in the same place" (1983, 4). Dowie wonders why Ford did not place the gas tank over the rear axle, Ford's patented design for its Capri models. This placement is confirmed by Dowie, Velasquez, and some Ford engineers as the "safest place." Yet, according to Davidson and Goodpaster, other studies at Ford showed that the Capri placement actually increased the likelihood of ignition inside the automobile (1983, 4). Moreover, such placement reduces storage space and precludes a hatchback design. Velasquez says that "[b]ecause the Pinto was a rush project, styling preceded engineering" (Velasquez, 1988, 120), thus accounting for the gas tank placement. This notion may have been derived from Dowie's quotation, allegedly from a "Ford engineer, who doesn't want his name used," that "[t]his company is run by salesmen, not engineers; so the priority is styling, not safety" (1977a, 23).

Dowie claims that in addition to rushing the Pinto into production, "Ford engineers discovered in pre-production crash tests that rear-end collisions would rupture the Pinto's fuel system extremely easily" (1977a, 18). According to Dowie, Ford crash-tested the Pinto in a secret location, and in every test made at over 25 mph the fuel tank ruptured. But according to Ford, Pinto's gas tank exploded during many of its tests, because, following government guidelines, Ford had tested the car using a fixed barrier standard, wherein the vehicle is towed backwards into a fixed barrier at the speed specified in the test. Ford argued that Pinto behaved well under a less stringent moving-barrier standard, which, Ford contended, is a more realistic test (Davidson and Goodpaster, 1983; *State of Indiana v. Ford Motor Company*, 1979).

Ford Motor Company and the commentators on this case agree that in 1971, before Ford launched the automobile, an internal study showed that a rubber bladder inner tank would improve the reliability of Pinto's gas tank placement. The bladder would cost perhaps $5.08 (Dowie, 1977a, 29; Schmitt and May, 1979, 1023), $5.80 (Davidson and Goodpaster, 1983), or $11 (Velasquez, 1988, 120). The $11 figure probably refers to a design adjustment required to meet a later government rollover standard. However, the idea of this installation was discarded, according to Ford, because of the unreliability of the rubber at cold temperatures, a conjecture not mentioned by commentators. Dowie also contends that Ford could have reduced the dangers from rear-end collisions by installing a $1 plastic baffle between the gas tank and the differential housing to reduce the likelihood of gas tank perforation. I can find no other verification of this contention.

All commentators claim that Ford did a cost/benefit analysis to determine whether it would be more costly to change the Pinto design or to assume the liability costs for burn victims, and memos to that effect were cited as evidence at the Grimshaw trial (*Grimshaw v. Ford Motor Co.,* 1978, 570). However, according to trial evidence submitted by Ford in *Grimshaw,* this estimate was made in 1973, the year *after* the Grimshaw accident, after Ford had evaluated a proposed new government rollover standard. According to evidence presented by Ford in *Grimshaw,* Ford calculated that it would cost $11 per auto to meet the rollover requirement. Ford used government data for the cost of a life ($200,000 per person), and projected an estimate of 180 burn deaths from rollovers. The study was not applicable to rear-end collisions, as some commentators, following Dowie's story, claimed.

Many reports of this case noted the $200,000 figure as Ford's price of a human life. Dowie says, for example, "Ever wonder what your life is worth in dollars? Perhaps $10 million? Ford has a better idea: $200,000" (1977a, 24). In fact, it was the National Highway Traffic Safety Administration's 1973 figure.

How many people have died as a result of being inside a Pinto during a rear-end collision? "By conservative estimates Pinto crashes have caused 500 burn deaths to people who would not have been seriously injured had the car not burst into flames. The figure could be as high as 900," Dowie claimed (1977a, 18). Hoffman repeats Dowie's figures, word for word (1984, 133). A more cautious Velasquez claims that by 1978 at least 53 people had died and "many more had been severely burnt" (Velasquez, 1988, 122). Schmitt and May, quoting a 1978 article in an issue of *Business and Society Review* that I could not find, estimate the number as "at least 32" (1979, 1024, and 1024 at note 16). Davidson and Goodpaster claim that by 1978, NHTSA estimated that 38 cases involved 27 fatalities (1983, 5).

In the 1978 trial that followed the Grimshaw accident, a jury awarded Grimshaw at least $125 million in punitive damages. *Auto News* printed a headline, "Ford Fights Pinto Case: Jury Gives 128 Million" on February 13, 1978. The commonly cited figure of $125 million is in the court records as the total initial punitive award. The $128 million might be the total award including punitive damages. This award was later reduced on appeal to $3.5 million, a fact that is seldom cited.

A second famous Pinto accident led Indiana to charge Ford with criminal liability. Hoffman reports the incident that led to the charges, on which all agree:

On August 10, 1978, a tragic automobile accident occurred on US Highway 33 near Goshen, Indiana. Sisters Judy and Lynn Ulrich (ages 18 and
16, respectively) and their cousin Donna Ulrich (age 18) were struck from
the rear in their 1973 Ford Pinto by a van. The gas tank of the Pinto ruptured, the car burst into flames, and the three teenagers were burned to
death. (1984, 132)

There are two points of interest in this case that apparently led the jury
to find Ford not guilty. First, in June 1978 Ford recalled 1.5 million Pintos in order to modify the fuel tank. There was some evidence that the
Ulrich auto had not participated in the recall (*State of Indiana v. Ford Motor Company,* 1979). Second, Ulrich's Pinto was hit from behind at 50
mph by a van driven by a man named Duggar. Duggar later testified that
he looked down for a "smoke" and then hit the car, although, according
to police reports, the Ulrich car had safety blinkers on. Found in Duggar's van were at least two empty beer bottles and an undisclosed
amount of marijuana. Yet this evidence, cited in the *State of Indiana v.
Ford Motor Co.* case, is seldom mentioned in the context of the Ulrich
tragedy, and Duggar was never indicted.

The purpose of this exercise is not to exonerate Ford or to argue for
bringing back the Pinto. Rather, it is to point out a simple phenomenon—a story can become a narrative and can be taken as fact even when
other alleged equally verifiable facts contradict that story. Moreover, one
narrative can dominate as *the facts.* Dowie's interesting tale of the Pinto
became the prototype for Pinto cases; many authors accepted his version
without going back to check whether his data were correct or to question
why some of his data contradicted Ford and government claims. Dowie's
reporting of Grimshaw became a prototype for the narrative of the Ulrich
case as well, so that questions concerning the recall of the Ulrich auto
and Duggar's performance were virtually ignored. Such omissions not
only make Ford look better, they also question the integrity of these reports and cases. Thus, this set of cases illustrates pitfalls that develop
when a particular narrative becomes the paradigm for data and fact.

THE DOW CORNING CORPORATION (DCC) BREAST IMPLANT CONTROVERSIES

Let me outline another set of narratives, those revolving around the
more recent DCC silicone breast implant controversies. I begin with a
narrative told by a number of protagonists in the case.

In 1943 DCC was formed by Dow Chemical Company and Corning
Glass, and it is still owned and controlled by these two corporations. It
was created to focus research and development on silicone, a series of

materials made from silicon, newly discovered to be an almost inert element with a vast number of potential uses in industry and medicine. There are at least 1,000 types of silicone, and today various forms of silicone are used in pacemakers, shunts, and hypodermic needles, as well as in nearly 5,000 industrial products (Dyer et al., 1995; Stocker, Gorman, and Werhane, 1997).

Beginning in 1962, DCC developed and manufactured breast implants, filled with silicone gel, and in 1975 it changed the design of the implant to a thinner shell that, according to the company, was more "natural," thus less likely to harden over time. Usually considered the leader in the field, DCC is the largest of a number of silicone implant manufacturers, which, until recently, included Bristol Myers Squibb, Baxter, and 3M.

According to DCC (and records of the company confirm this) the first and second implants were extensively tested on animals before being manufactured. But DCC and the other manufacturers of breast implants did not conduct or sponsor any epidemiological studies on implant recipients until the 1990s. They did not keep track on who had received implants or trace their medical history. Indeed, it is uncertain how many women have actually received silicone implants since their first manufacture.

Until 1989, the Food and Drug Administration (FDA) had no testing or safety protocols for implants of any kind, so testing was not required for these and other implant devices before manufacture. The safety check was not required, because it had been determined that silicone was a safe material (thus, it was assumed the products made from silicone were safe for implantation). Prior to 1990 there had been few complaints from implant recipients about the product, even from those whose implants had ruptured (Dyer et al., 1995).

When DCC began to produce this product, it developed brochures for physicians and surgeons explaining the possible negative side effects of breast implants: inflammation, scarring, local discomfort, hardening of the implants, and rupture. Potential recipients of implants were to be informed by their surgeon about these dangers. According to studies on informed consent, when implant devices of all sorts were first developed, it was customary to inform the physicians and surgeons, relying on them to adequately inform their patients (Swazey, 1996). Patients were seldom informed directly by implant manufacturers about the risks of those products. Sometime between 1962 and 1990 this custom changed, and now potential recipients of implants expect the manufacturer of the devices, as well as their physicians, to give them information about the devices and their potential dangers. Since 1985, DCC has created pamphlets to be distributed directly to potential recipients and implant patients by the physician or surgeon.

Until 1990 DCC received very few complaints about its breast implants and was subject to only two major lawsuits, although at least one third of all implants harden or rupture over time (Dyer et al., 1995). Between 1992 and 1995, out of the approximately 2 million women who have had implants, at least 440,000 joined class action suits or brought individual lawsuits claiming to have experienced a variety of illnesses as a result of their implants, including autoimmune diseases such as lupus and rheumatoid arthritis, connective tissues diseases, scleroderma, cancer, and other illnesses such as pain, fatigue, insomnia, memory loss, and headaches. (Angell, 1996; Kolata, 1995a, C1, C6; Kolata and Meier, 1995, A1).

In 1992 Dr. David Kessler, commissioner of the FDA, banned breast implant surgery except for medical reasons.[1] Kessler (1992) defended his decision by claiming that manufacturers of these implants had not sufficiently proved their safety.

The first epidemiological studies of breast implants were not conducted until the early 1990s. An epidemiological study is designed to test a certain hypothesis, in this case, the hypothesis that women with silicone breast implants are more likely to develop certain diseases than those without implants (Angell, 1996, 92). In these particular studies, the medical history of women with implants is compared to the medical history of similar women who have not had the surgery to determine whether there is a higher incidence of disease, or of a particular set of diseases, in either group. The two most well-known and, according to experts, most reliable studies were conducted by the Mayo Clinic and the National Institutes of Health (NIH) with Brigham Women's Hospital. The Mayo Clinic study of 749 women "found no association between breast implants and the connective tissue diseases and other disorders we studied" (Gabriel, cited in Angell, 1996, 90). A more extensive study, conducted by Brigham Women's Hospital, examined the records of 87,318 female nurses from the ages of 30 to 55, covering their medical records over a 14-year span. This study, partly funded by the NIH is the basis for a larger study of 450,000 women. This study found only a very weak connection between implants and scleroderma, rheumatoid arthritis, lupus, and connective tissue disease. "The maximum risk is about 1.2, meaning that [f]or every 10 women *without* implants who develop connective tissue disease [for example], 12 women *with* implants in an equal population would develop it" (Angell, 1996, 196).

Nevertheless, based on research conducted by Dr. Nir Kossovsky, a few researchers at UCLA Medical Center and Mark Lappé, assert persuasively that there is a significantly higher level of autoimmune disease in women with implants (Kossovsky, 1993, 281–8; 1994, 237–46; Lappé, 1993, 348–52).

According to at least one report (Castleman, 1998, 6) at least one third to one half of all implants rupture or leak within 10 years. In 1997 a study conducted by FDA official Louise Brinton with S. Lori Brown of the National Cancer Institute (NCI) concluded that, although implants frequently leak and rupture, there is only the slightest statistical link between connective tissue disease and leaking implants. "These diseases are so rare that it may never be possible to clearly link them to silicone breast implants," Dr. Brown concluded (Brinton and Brown, 1997, 1349).

Although this is an evolving case insufficient to yield exhaustive comparisons, we can profitably focus on three questions. First, do silicone breast implants cause cancer and other diseases, in particular connective tissue or autoimmune diseases? Second, did the industry, and DCC in particular, cover up or not inform physicians or female patients about the risks of implantation. Third, did DCC fail to acknowledge and promptly investigate problems with its implants? The answers to these questions are not simple because of the variety of narratives that dominate this controversy.

The first question is the most puzzling. According to Kossovsky and Lappé, silicone breast implants can affect the immune system and harm the system acutely when an implant ruptures (Taubes, 1995). However, a seldom-cited fact in the case is that pacemakers and a number of other implant devices are also made from silicone. Yet pacemaker wearers have not sued for illnesses that allegedly result from that implant. The difference is that breast implants tend to rupture over time, leaking silicone throughout the system; pacemakers do not.

Numerous independent epidemiological studies have been unable to establish any correlation between breast implants and cancer. Data shows that there is only a weak correlation between implants, even those that have leaked, and connective tissue disease, or autoimmune diseases (Giltay et al., 1994; McLaughlin and Fraumeni, 1994; Sánchez-Guerrero et al., 1995). According to these findings, at worst, there is a statistical possibility that breast implants cause one additional case per 3,000 women of an autoimmune disease per year (Angell, 1996). An overwhelming number of physicians and other scientists interpret the evidence to indicate that implants do not, as a rule, cause disease or, at least, any known disease.

Nevertheless, a number of lawsuits in which experts such as Kossovsky have testified have been won by claimants who argued that they became ill because of their implants. In 1991 the largest damages, $7.3 million, were awarded to Mariann Hopkins, who claimed to have become ill from her DCC implant. It appears, then, that the views of a few researchers and physicians and the testimony of ill women with implants have counted as the most persuasive evidence in a number of court cases.

The second question about a cover-up of evidence is also puzzling.

The company claims that it did not and points out that independent studies of silicone repeatedly demonstrate its safety and that DCC instigated its own studies that found no conclusive link between silicone and disease. From 1962 until about 1990, DCC tested silicone extensively but tested the implants themselves only secondarily. Based on the inert nature of silicone, DCC predicted few complications. And there were few complaints from implant patients about the product, but DCC did not communicate directly with patients.

From the very beginning DCC informed physicians and surgeons about the risks of implants, including the likelihood of rupture or hardening in some patients. Brochures were distributed to the surgeons but not directly to potential patients until 1985. Did DCC fail to recognize changes in the custom of informed consent that mandated patient information? Did DCC assume that surgeons performing implant surgery were all reasonable and responsible professionals who would inform their patients uniformly and thoroughly about the risks of implantation (Flax and Werhane, 1997)?

The third question about DCC's failure to acknowledge and promptly investigate problems with implants would be moot if implants do not cause serious diseases. Yet more is at stake here. It and other silicone breast implant manufacturers depended on the narratives of science and technology. Managers at DCC are primarily engineers and scientists, who more than likely concluded that if silicone was an inert substance, then implants made of silicone were also harmless. They presumably conjectured that only scientific evidence would count as evidence in the courts. They may have assumed that the media would not print a story to the contrary when such scientific evidence appeared to be conclusive, or that the courts and juries would not accept as *overriding* evidence what an overwhelming majority of scientists consider very weak contrary data and testimony of ill implant recipients.

According to Marcia Angell, an editor of the *New England Journal of Medicine* and an expert on breast implants, DCC's assumptions are based on the well-grounded belief that "[i]n science, the requirement for verifiable evidence must be met, no matter who the researchers are or what their credentials" (Angell, 1996, 94). Assuming that the matter was one of science, DCC may have failed to recognize that the emotional traumas of women with implants who become ill would frame the issues and judgments about the dangers of breast implants. It is no wonder that DCC could not figure out how it became the target for litigation, because DCC focused primarily on what it concluded to be adequate scientific evidence.

In 1992, because of the series of new cases that alleged a causal connection between implants and disease, the FDA withdrew silicone breast implants from the market except for specified medical uses. According to the FDA, breast implants were not withdrawn from the market because they were proven to be harmful, but because the FDA concluded that the evidence was not strong enough to show they were *not* harmful (US Food and Drug Administration, 1991, 49098–9). The FDA's philosophy, or at least the philosophy of its director, Dr. David Kessler, who ordered the withdrawal, raises a question about the role of scientific evidence. How much evidence is needed to demonstrate beyond a reasonable doubt that a product is not harmful? What is meant by "beyond a reasonable doubt"? How much is "sufficient evidence"? Clearly Kessler and DCC scientists have different perspectives, or mental models, about the "measure of reasonable doubt."

Another set of media narratives also describe the emotional reactions of ill women, the dominating one being *Business Week*'s cover story article, "Informed Consent" (Byrne, 1995a) from which John Byrne's book (1995b) of the same title was produced. Byrne dwells on the emotional trauma of Colleen Swanson, the wife of a DCC manager, John Swanson, who had recently resigned from the company after 27 years of employment. Swanson's position at DCC is unclear. He is sometimes cited as the ethics officer. Even though he was the only permanent member of the Ethics Committee (a committee that had been functioning since the 1970s), DCC claims never to have had an official "ethics officer."

Colleen Swanson had implants 17 years ago and has been suffering from a variety of illnesses almost since the end of the operation. Describing Colleen's condition before she had the implants removed, Bryne writes:

> In the evening, at home, Colleen was slipping closer to what seemed like a slow death. Her breasts had become increasingly hard and painful. Nearly unbearable pain convulsed her left arm, hand, and ring and index fingers. Her fatigue grew worse and her interest in sex decreased. By March 1991, the pain moved into her hips and the mobility of both the right and left sides of her body declined. The ache spread to her neck and became so intense she could barely hold up her head (1995, 139).

Byrne cites the epidemiological evidence, but undercuts it as follows:

> Recent studies from Harvard Medical School and the Mayo Clinic, among others, have cast doubt on the link between implants and disease. But critics have attacked these studies on numerous grounds—among them that they look only for recognized diseases such as lupus, rather than the complex of ailments many recipients complain of. (1995b, 116)

One of the interesting elements of the case is the "after this therefore because of this" fallacy: women with implants are ill; therefore, implants caused the illnesses. Most scientists would argue that a correlation between x and y does not, by itself, demonstrate a causal link. So in this series of cases causality itself, on which much of science is grounded, seems to be brought into question. The dominating emotional narratives, particularly Bryne's, have often overshadowed the scientific ones, so that even the contradictory nature of these conflicting stories does not surface as an issue.

We have before us a number of narratives: the epidemiological evidence, the narratives of scientific causality, DCC's testing practices, DCC's perception of the validity and completeness of this testing and informed consent procedures, and women with implants who are ill. Despite fresh scientific data that further question the connection between implants and disease (Brinton and Brown, 1997; Carey, 1996), the Byrne narrative and narratives of ill women with breast implants continue to preoccupy public opinion about DCC and the dangers of implants. As in *Rashomon,* the storytellers are believed, but the truth underlying this set of narratives remains unresolved. This example illustrates how apparently contradictory narratives can both operate in a particular situation. It also illustrates the power of a narrative based on, or appealing to, emotion, a phenomenon that cannot be disregarded, because those narratives function as versions of the truth.

THE SALOMON BROTHERS TREASURY
BOND INCIDENTS

The Salomon Brothers Treasury bond incidents reveal how narratives play distorting roles both in public perception and in self-perception. The incidents, as they are retold, also illustrate how narratives can function as creative explanatory mechanisms when no other viable explanation is forthcoming. None of the stories about Salomon Brothers bond trading practices can be confirmed as true or false, none can be verified as approximating actuality, none can be agreed upon, and each may or may not reflect the thinking of those involved in these events.

What is known about the Salomon Brothers incidents is the following:

Salomon Brothers is one of 40 investment and commercial banks which are primary bidders on Treasury bonds, and Salomon is one of the three largest purchasers. Preceding the Treasury Bond incidents that made the front pages in 1991, Salomon had been cited a number of times for SEC trading violations, although they were merely fined a small amount, and no one was prosecuted. According to Treasury regulations, no bond trader can bid on more than 35% of the bonds offered at any one Treasury securities issue. Apparently, according to reports, during the years 1990 and 1991 Paul Mozer, the head of Government bond trading at Salomon, made large bids in customers' names (a) about which the customers were not informed and (b) which, totaled with Salomon's own legitimate ones, exceeded the 35% cap. Treasury bonds are offered for sale every three months, and these excessive bids, along with Salomon's own allowed Salomon to dominate the bond market on at least three occasions, so that it could negotiate and, or was in a position to negotiate and create premiums for the prices of those bonds. Evidence suggests that three senior officers at Salomon, John Gutfreund, the Chairman, John Meriwether, vice chairman, and Thomas Strauss, the president knew about these irregularities as early as February 1991, but failed to report the violations to the SEC (nor changed the practices of Mozer, the chief bond trader) until May of that year.

Eventually, Warren Buffett, a majority stockholder of Salomon Brothers, fired Gutfreund, Meriwether, and Strauss as well as Mozer, and canceled their year-end bonuses. (See Bartlett, 1991, C1; Murray, 1991, A1.)

The Salomon Brothers case raises questions of why. Why did Paul Mozer, Salomon's chief government bond trader, deliberately flaunt Treasury Department regulations, some of which were written to control traders like him? Why did the head of Salomon, John Gutfreund, and other senior Salomon executives, keep silent after discovering improprieties in Salomon's trading activities? Given the continued media attention to ethical issues, and the popular focus on Salomon by Michael Lewis in his 1989 best-selling book *Liar's Poker,* why was this firm not more alert and more careful, particularly when engaging in activities likely to draw public attention? All players in this case had more to lose monetarily and in reputation by such trading and nonreporting, the firm was doing well, and none of the participants needed money. So the case is intriguing, but not because of what transpired or the illegality and impropriety of the actions, nor because of the gains to be made with such trading. Rather, one wonders why, in the climate of highly visible media exposure and in the engagement of large transactions with a government agency, would anyone *consider* violating Treasury rules or imagine that such violations would not be detected.

One popular narrative about Salomon Brothers is depicted in *Liar's Poker.* According to Michael Lewis, the book's author, Liar's Poker was a popular game at Salomon:

> In Liar's Poker a group of people—as few as two, as many as ten—form a circle. Each player holds a dollar bill close to his chest. The game is similar in spirit to the card game known as I Doubt It. Each Player attempts to fool the others about the serial numbers printed on the face of his dollar bill. One trader begins by making "a bid." He says, for example, "Three sixes." He means that all told the serial numbers of the dollar bills held by every player, including himself, contain at least three sixes. . . . The player to the left of the bidder can do one of two things. He can bid higher. . . . Or he can "challenge"—that is like saying "I doubt it."
> The bidding escalates until all the other players agree to challenge a single player's bid. Then, and only then, do the players reveal their serial numbers and determine who is bluffing whom. (1989, 16)

Lewis contends that the game illustrated the corporate culture at Salomon at that time, particularly among the bond traders, thought to be the "elite" of the company, who made a great deal of money and thus influenced the power center at Salomon. According to Lewis, while the chairman, vice chairman, and president ran the company and held the power, they virtually left each bond trader alone so long as he or she was producing revenue. Despite this individualism and independence, there were strong mores and customs at Salomon that set the standards for behavior. Starting traders were introduced to the corporate culture at the management training sessions, where they were expected to be rowdy and challenging. As starting traders they were treated with disdain and verbally abused, treated as "idiots," and expected to produce or be fired. The bond trading floor was like a jungle and "a trader is a savage, and a great trader a great savage" (Lewis, 1989, 41). There was virtually no respect for persons other than high producers, and one could come into or go out of respect depending on one's ability to continue to be profitable. This was obviously a male-dominated society, and women had no place as bond traders. Explicit sexual language was common, the most famous expression being "a big swinging dick," referring to a trader who had managed to become successful through telephone trading. In addition to aggressive trading, according to Lewis, it was common for bond traders to exploit customers by selling them loss-leaders such as bonds owned by Salomon thought to be overvalued. In priority, Lewis contends, Salomon Brothers placed itself as the primary stakeholder to whom it was responsible; second, it valued its traders; customers were a distant third, at least on the bond trading floor. It is no wonder, then, if Lewis's narrative is at all plausible, if this was a dominant movie running on the bond trading floor at Salomon Brothers, that Paul Mozer would believe his task to be as aggressive as possible in the Treasury bond market.

But, was Lewis's description of Salomon accurate, or does his story create "fact"? Maybe Mozer himself read the book and believed its story.

Mozer's trading activities may have been even more bizarre than Lewis's description can account for. According to some reports, Mozer was determined to beat the Treasury at its game of rules. He seemed to be obsessed with the Treasury Department as an opponent as though he was in a world championship chess match. According to one Treasury official, "He thought he was bigger than the US Treasury" (Bartlett, 1991, C1). One way to try to comprehend Mozer's actions is to describe his activities as part of a narrative he created from the Salomon culture, the rules of which are to win, despite legal and moral side effects. Unless one argues that Mozer was an inherently evil person, a view for which there is *no* evidence, one way to account for his behavior is to propose that he saw himself almost exclusively in a strongly differentiated role as a trader. What was required as a trader took moral precedence over other demands. His primary aim, according to this explanation, was to acquire and trade as many Treasury bonds as possible. Mozer may have had little perspective on who he was or what he was doing outside of that narrative. One could almost believe that he imagined the Treasury Department as a player who saw bond trading as he did: a challenge with opponents, the goal of which is to outmaneuver the opponent with whatever strategy is necessary. Did Mozer create his own narrative and lose track of the status of his opponent? Did he, for instance, forget about the power of the law that backed the Treasury Department?

A third set of narratives could explain the behavior of Mozer and the top managers at Salomon. Mozer, Gutfreund, Strauss, and Meriwether may all, in different ways, suffer from a Camelot complex. In Camelot everything seemed to be perfect, and some people in Camelot, even perhaps King Arthur himself, believed it was an ideal place, but of course, in fact, it was not (Schwartz, 1987). Salomon Brothers was a highly successful firm. It has survived bad times on Wall Street, it had not suffered during the junk bond slump, and the accusations in *Liar's Poker* either had not been substantiated or had not tainted the firm to its customers or to the Treasury Department, which gave it privileged status as one of the select primary dealers of Treasury bonds. Perhaps, then, at least unconsciously, these people at Salomon developed a of cult of narcissism. Mozer, for example, was highly successful at the bond auctions; he might have felt he could not fail. He became an ideal, a cult figure other bond traders emulated. Life at Salomon Brothers was like that in Camelot. Camelot, like Salomon Brothers, eventually ran into difficulties precipitated by preoccupation with the invulnerability of its own tale (Schwartz, 1987).

These of narratives about Salomon Brothers' bond trading floor and Treasury bond scandal are in some sense self-referential. They create a "reality" that may or may not describe Salomon's bond trading floor, Paul Mozer's motives, or what happened to precipitate the events. Both interesting and frightening, each of these narratives "fits" as an explanation. Each of them presents a believable account; yet, while functioning as coherent explanatory models, their veracity is unknown. Thus, this example, unlike the others, shows the believability of a logically viable explanatory narrative or set of narratives, even where there is no evidence to justify the descriptions or allegations.

SOME LIMITS OF NARRATIVES

What can we say about the role of narratives? Conditioned, but not determined by background narratives, each of us orders, selects, structures, and even censors all our experiences. These shaping mechanisms are mental models through which we experience the world, and we never see the world except through points of view, models, or framing mechanisms, some of which shape background and other more specific narratives. Indeed, narratives that shape our experiences and influence how we think about the world are essential to the coherence of our experiences. As I have just illustrated, some narratives are more closely based on actual experiences; others are taken from the narratives of others that we have accepted as true; still others are closer to fiction. In any case, some narratives influence, dominate, or reshape our thinking about certain events. Dowie's portrayal of the Pinto case became the prototype for other case descriptions. Bryne's narrative of the Swansons may soon take on that role, and *Liar's Poker* for some time was believed to describe the reality at Salomon Brothers. Meanwhile, Mozer's narrative of Salomon may have become for Mozer the only point of view that he recognized. In these instances "life imitates art," or the "grammar," the alleged data of the narrative, creates the essence of the story that becomes fact for a number of its participants, readers, listeners, or the media. Numbers of Pinto cases have imitated Dowie's account so that account becomes "life"—the "truth" about Ford's development and marketing of the Pinto. Byrne's story of Colleen Swanson has become an appealing narrative that overshadows other accounts by DCC, scientists, physicians, and Marcia Angell.

Does this mean that one can never arrive at facts or truths? Yes and no. A longer answer requires explanation. The thesis that experience is always framed by a perspective or point of view is closely related to another thesis discussed in the last chapter, that "[*e*]*ssence* is expressed by grammar" (Wittgenstein, 1953, §371). In short, as I argued in an earlier chapter, our experiences are framed, organized, and made meaningful only through language. To put the point in more Kantian terms, the "stuff" of our experience is not created or made up (although sometimes we can and do make up the content of our experiences when we envelop ourselves in fantasy). The distinction between reality and fantasy may be that we do not make up the content of our experience. Nevertheless, that stuff, or phenomena, is never pure—it is always constituted and contaminated by our perspective, narrative, point of view, or mental models. Are we, then, trapped in these narratives?

One way to think about narratives is to appeal to Amartya Sen's concept of positional objectivity. Because narratives represent a collection of congruent points of view that others share or can share, they are, or can be, "positionally objective":

> What we can observe depends on our position vis-à-vis the objects of observation. . . . Positionally dependent observations, beliefs, and actions are central to our knowledge and practical reason. The nature of objectiv-

ity in epistemology, decision theory, and ethics has to take adequate note of the parametric dependence of observation and inference on the position of the observer. (Sen, 1993, 126)

Position-dependency defines the way in which the object appears "from a delineated somewhere." This delineated somewhere, however, is positionally objective. That is, any person in that position will make similar observations, according to Sen. Sen assumes that from a certain point of view we are able to observe and process the same data similarly. I would add that the parameters of positionality are not merely spatial but involve a shared mental model. For example, managers at Ford had access to much of the same data about the Pinto and approached the Pinto accidents from a positionally dependent point of view. Ford's decision not to recall the Pinto, despite some terrible accidents, could be defended as a positionally objective belief based on the ways in which managers at Ford processed information on automobile crashes. Other managers at Ford would probably have adopted that point of view as well. Outsiders, however—for example, Pinto owners—might have processed the same information differently, for instance, if they operated under a belief system that placed safety concerns ahead of economy. These two perspectives are analogous to the views of the Copernicans and Ptolemains, who at least initially processed the same data about the universe, but each processed it differently, resulting in different conclusions and thus conflicting positionally objective points of view.

Dow Corning's reluctance to stop manufacturing silicone implants could be construed as positionally objective from its focus on scientific evidence and reliance on responsible surgeons to inform patients about the possible dangers of implants. Colleen Swanson and other ill recipients of implants also adapt a positionally objective view from their perspective as very ill people with implants. In fact, DCC and implant recipients have difficulty communicating with each other, because they approach the case and the facts of the case from different positionally objective perspectives.

However, a positionally objective point of view could be mistaken if it did not account for all available information. Sen points out that in almost all cases no one need unconditionally accept a positionally objective view. Almost any position has alternatives; almost every position has its critics. I would qualify that further. Allegedly, positionally objective phenomena are still phenomena that have been filtered through the social sieve of a shared mental model or narrative, neither infallible nor complete.

According to Sen, in addition to taking positionally objective points of view, we are able to engage in "transpositional" assessments or what Sen has called a constructed view from nowhere. A transpositional view from nowhere is a constructed critique of a positionally objective phenomenon, and no positionally objective view is merely relative or im-mune from challenge. This assessment compares various positionally objective points of view to determine whether one can make coherent sense of them and develop some general theories about what is being observed. From a transpositional point of view, mental models them-selves can be questioned on the basis of their coherence or their ex-planatory scope. Transpositional assessments are *constructed* views, be-cause they too depend on the schemas of the assessors. Although the challenge could be conducted only from another mental model, the as-sessment could take into account a variety of points of view. Still, revi-sions of the schema in question might produce another mental model that more comprehensively explained a range of phenomena or inci-dents. In short, studying sets of perspectives can show how certain events are experienced and reported and even the mental models or narratives at work in shaping the narratives about these experiences. Al-though one can never begin with a pure tabula rasa, nevertheless one can, at least in principle, achieve a limited, dispassionate perspective.

But if a constructed view from somewhere is a possibility, why, then, do we observe so many instances when people have failed to critique their situation from a more dispassionate or alternate perspective? Just as some of us fail to evaluate our roles, role obligations, and the institu-tions to which these roles are attached, so too, we often fail to evaluate what we take to be an objective point of view, and seldom do we think about the mental model or movie with which we frame our situation. A constructed view from *somewhere* is a metaphysical possibility, realizable only when one has a sense of the shortcomings of one's situation, that is, when one has a very active moral imagination.

Near the end of *Rashomon,* the narrator of the tale, the passerby, laments society's lack of trust resulting from the impossibility of ascertaining truth. Our mental models and the narratives in which we embed our lives and our activities must be examined and evaluated often and with care. In coming into contact with others' narratives, one should not de-pend on a single set of alleged facts or data as presented in their stories. Rather, we need to examine how the facts are constituted to make a story or a case, and one realize that some of those cases can become pro-totypical narratives that we imitate. The "classic cases" need to be revis-ited or they will become clichéd prototypes. We need also to be wary of assumptions generated by these prototypes, such as the assumption that Dow Corning caused egregious harm, perhaps even deliberately, to the more than 440,000 women who claim to be ill from its breast implants, or the assumption that what scientists accept as adequate evidence tells the whole story. Although we cannot arrive at The Truth, we can at least approximate well-grounded beliefs and distinguish them from myth and fantasy. Otherwise, we will find ourselves in a postmodern world illustrated by the Salomon stories, where fantasizing takes over, and the narratives we create take on the guise of reality (Vargish, 1991). In the next two chapters I examine in detail this process of developing well-grounded beliefs in the context of moral imagination.

5

Moral Imagination

In the late 1970s the pharmaceutical company Merck developed a highly successful antiparasitic drug, called ivermectin, used for attacking worms and other parasites in animals. After testing this drug extensively on a number of animal parasites, the leading researcher on ivermectin, Dr. William Campbell, concluded that a version of ivermectin might also be successful in combating onchocerciasis, or "river blindness." River blindness, a disease spread by black flies that breed near rivers, is caused by a parasite worm inflicted by a fly bite. The worms multiply under the skin, causing terrible itching and eventually blinding its human victims. Approximately 18 million people have river blindness, and almost 100 million are in danger of becoming infected. Unfortunately, almost all of these people live in very poor countries in remote areas of the world.

Campbell approached the head of research at Merck, Roy Vagolos, and Vagolos and Campbell realized that if this drug were developed, the customer base would be almost exclusively people in developing countries where river blindness was prevalent. These customers had no income, and the countries in which they lived include the poorest in the world. Ordinarily it takes about 10 years and up to $350 million to develop and perfect a drug for humans, and ordinarily Merck did not proceed with a drug that did not have a promised customer base of at least $20 million per year. Yet the effectiveness of ivermectin in animals encouraged Vagolos to allow Campbell and his researchers to proceed with this research. Both men thought that somewhere in the process some global relief agency would help fund the development and subsequent manufacture of the drug if it was successful.

After almost 10 years, a successful version of ivermectin for humans, called Mectizan, was developed. Merck had thought all along that if it developed a successful product, WHO or some other international or US organization would help fund the development, testing, manufacture, and distribution of the drug. However, WHO had just invested several million dollars in fly eradication in countries with large river blindness infections without success, and was unwilling to invest further money even to test the drug. No other agency came forward. So Merck initiated and funded drug testing in human subjects.

Mectizan proved to be highly successful. It arrested the growth of river blindness in victims infected with the parasite and prevented it from occurring when given to children. Producing the drug was relatively inexpensive, and one could simply take one pill a year in order for the drug to be effective.

Still, even at $1 a dosage, no organization was willing to help Merck in funding the drug. So Merck decided to give the drug away. Its next problem was distribution, because neither those infected with river blindness nor their governments were capable of administering Mectizan. Setting up distribution channels in remote areas was a complex task. Finally helped by international organizations, Merck instigated a 12-year program to distribute the drug. At the end of 1995 Merck had succeeded in giving away over 19 million doses of Mectizan. Merck plans to continue this project indefinitely (Bollier, 1996, 280–94; Bollier, Weiss, and Hanson, 1991).

In *Aiming Higher* (1996), David Bollier cites companies such as Merck "in which creative, socially committed business managers have enhanced their long-term profitability by instilling the best of their humanity into the nitty-gritty operations of their organizations" (1). According to Bollier, these companies have a "questing spirit . . . [or] moral imagination" (1996, 2). In this chapter I examine the question of moral imagination. While I do not argue that *all* moral reasoning is grounded in the imagination, I conclude that moral imagination is a necessary ingredient in responsible moral judgment. Only through imagination can one project alternate ways to frame experience and thus broaden, evaluate, and even change one's moral point of view.

Let us begin with some stipulative definitions of imagination and moral imagination. Philosophers have long been interested in the phenomenon of imagination. Many philosophers once thought that imagination was a particular psychological faculty that accounts not merely for our abilities to represent or create mental images but also for our creation and appreciation of aesthetic objects. Later, Adam Smith (1759/1976) believed imagination to be a faculty that enables us to understand the sentiments of others. Immanuel Kant (1790/1951) said that imagination accounts for the ways in which the mind synthesizes sensations and perceptions to form experiences and relates experiences to the understanding. Imagination is usually distinguished from reason, for to be imaginative one need not be restricted by reason. But imagination is not necessarily merely subjective, for we share appreciation of imaginative works, such as works of art. Nor is imagination necessarily or intrinsically *irrational*. One can create imaginative representations of possible worlds that, though unreal, nevertheless have logic and consistency.

At its most basic level, imagination is the ability to form mental images of real or unreal phenomena or events and to develop different scenarios or different perspectives on those phenomena or events. Part of being imaginative is being creatively projective, creating new images or scenarios with known conceptual analogs. Imagination includes creating fantasies or myths. Paul Ricoeur once observed that "to imagine is to make oneself absent from the whole of things (1979, 152), to become disengaged, fragmented, focused on the fantastic, distanced from reality and ordinary experience. Imagination, then, can involve creating a fresh phenomenon, situation, or series of events (Beidelman, 1986, 1–10).

Moral imagination is a more slippery term, sometimes used in the management literature by writers such as Bollier to signal a morally courageous or unique activity or decision of a particular manager or company. Yet Bollier fails to *define* moral imagination except obliquely. Bollier does not clearly distinguish moral imagination from other forms of management decision-making except for his conclusion that morally imaginative managers and companies take on activities that extend the ordinary expectations for economic enterprises.

Edward Tivnan in *The Moral Imagination* (1995) uses the term to argue that controversial moral debates in our society, such as abortion, capital punishment, and racial justice, can be understood and even transcended if we, as an open democratic society, develop moral imagination. Quoting John Dewey, who said that "[i]magination is the chief instrument of the good" (1958, 348), Tivnan defines moral imagination as "imaginative sympathy" (253), "moral creativity" (250), or the ability to take an "imaginative leap" (252), allowing one to be "a decent, compassionate, good person in a diverse community" (249). Yet these definitions are not fully developed in Tivnan's book, and it is unclear from reading Tivnan how moral imagination is distinctively *moral* or how one develops moral imagination, either as an individual or as a society.

Moral imagination is a term widely used in literature and literary theory to talk about works that exemplify "paradigm[s] of moral activity" (Nussbaum 1990, 148) or that "draw analogies between the imaginary world [of the work of literature] and the world in which we live" (Guroian, 1996, 6). Moral imagination sometimes describes the approach an artist or novelist takes in developing material. For example, in *Forms of Life: Character and Moral Imagination in the Novel* (1983),

Martin Price argues that "moral imagination . . . is the depth and ade-
quacy of the novelist's conception of experience: the degree to which he
recognizes the complexities of decision or action or inaction and the ef-
fort or release involved in solving or ignoring or evading problems"
(xii). A work of literature may exhibit a depth of moral imagination, its
characters may exemplify moral imagination, or the work may stimulate
the moral imagination of its reader. Yet, surprisingly, while "moral imagination" is widely circulated in literary theory, it is seldom defined with
the clarity required for a good philosophical analysis.

Surprisingly, too, "moral imagination" is not well developed by many
moral philosophers. However, in a recent very fine book, *Moral Imagination* (1993), Mark Johnson defines moral imagination as "an ability to
imaginatively discern various possibilities for acting within a given situation and to envision the potential help and harm that are likely to result
from a given action" (202). Concerned with the limits of moral reasoning and moral judgment, in a recent article, the philosopher Charles
Larmore defines moral imagination as

> our ability to elaborate and appraise different courses of action which are
> only partially determined by the given content of moral rules, in order to
> learn what in a particular situation is the morally best thing to do. . . .
> Moral imagination belongs to . . . the exercise of moral judgment.
> (1981, 284–5)

Larmore questions the ability of moral rules, by themselves, to function
adequately in particular contexts, and he explicitly links moral imagination to situational moral judgments. Unfortunately, Larmore is less explicit about why and how situational moral judgments are imaginative.

Elaborating further on moral imagination, Martha Nussbaum claims
that "the work of the moral imagination is in some manner like the work
of the creative imagination" (1990, 148). Moral imagination enables
one

> to see more deeply into the relationship between fine-tuned perception of
> particulars and a rule-governed concern for general obligations: how
> each, taken by itself, is insufficient for moral accuracy, how (and why) the
> particular, if insufficient, is nonetheless prior; and how a dialogue be-
> tween the two . . . can find a common "basis" for moral judgment.
> (Nussbaum, 1990, 157)

Nussbaum's thoughts on moral imagination recall my arguments in
chapter 2 that moral awareness and moral judgment begin with the
particular—with a particular situation, temptation, or dilemma, because
it is in the context of social, particular situations that the thick self is embedded. Yet as critical thin selves we make rule-based judgments that en-
lighten, reshape, and sometimes resolve situational issues, temptations,
and dilemmas.

Merck's saga with Mectizan is a real-life example of this kind of dialogue. Vagolos perceived a "rule-governed concern for general obligations" to shareholders to develop profitable drugs. At the same time he was dealing with a "fine-tuned perception of particulars." His best researchers were on the verge of developing a revolutionary drug that could cure millions of people. Vagolos also remembered the words of George Merck, the son of Merck's founder: "We try never to forget that medicine is for the people. It is not for the profits. The profits follow, and if we have remembered that, they have never failed to appear. The better we have remembered it, the larger they have been" (Bollier, Weiss, and Hanson, 1991, A3). Given Campbell's research record in dialogue with George Merck's statement, Vagolos was able to break out of a mind-set or "rule-governed concern" that places developing drugs with a possible return of $20 million a year as the first priority. Vagolos took a creative and imaginative moral risk in approving the development of Mectizan, a risk that was a situational moral judgment but reinforced another "rule," George Merck's admonition that Merck's general obligation was "to the people." George Merck's statement illustrates what Archie Carroll means by moral imagination. One will recall from chapter 1 that Carroll defines moral imagination as "the ability to perceive that a web of competing economic relationships is, at the same time, a web of moral or ethical relationships" (1987, 13). George Merck, and later, Roy Vagelos, did not distinguish between two apparent missions at Merck: to develop medicines and to be profitable.

Moral imagination, then, is the ability in particular circumstances to discover and evaluate possibilities not merely determined by that circumstance, or limited by its operative mental models, or merely framed by a set of rules or rule-governed concerns. In managerial decision-making, moral imagination entails perceiving norms, social roles, and relationships entwined in any situation. Developing moral imagination involves heightened awareness of contextual moral dilemmas and their mental models, the ability to envision and evaluate new mental models that create new possibilities, and the capability to reframe the dilemma and create new solutions in ways that are novel, economically viable, and morally justifiable.

SOME ROOTS OF THE CONCEPTS OF MORAL IMAGINATION

One early proponent of a concept of moral imagination was the eighteenth-century philosopher and economist Adam Smith. In the first chapter of *Theory of Moral Sentiments* (*TMS*) (1759/1976), Smith argues that "[h]ow selfish soever man may be supposed, there are evidently some principles in his nature, which interest him in the fortune of others" (I.i.1.1). One of these "principles" is sympathy. At the same time, Smith says that "[a]s we have no immediate experience of what other men feel, we can form no idea of the manner in which they are affected, but by conceiving what we ourselves should feel in the like situation" (1759/1976, I.i.2).

In Smith's technical use of the term, sympathy is neither empathy nor any other sentiment or passion. Rather, it designates an agreement to or an understanding of the sentiments of another (1759/1976, I.i.1.5). When I sympathize, I place myself in another's situation, not because of how that situation feels to me or might affect me, but rather as if I were that person. I project myself into another's experience, according to Smith, in order to understand, although not vicariously experience, what another person is feeling, rather than merely to relate that situation to my own. Sympathy, then, is the recognition and comprehension of what another feels or might feel in a situation, but it is not an experiential, emotionally empathetic, or sentimental identification with that feeling. Thus, through sympathy I can cognitively understand the emotions of others without actually feeling them.

The role of imagination is crucial in understanding Smith's concept of sympathy and, indeed, his whole moral psychology. Smith claims that each of us has an active imagination, which enables us mentally to recreate another's feelings, passions, and point of view. In this imaginative process of sympathy one does not literally feel the passion of another; rather, one understands what another is experiencing from that person's perspective. Imagination is also useful in self-evaluation; it enables me to look at myself from the point of view of another person.

Imagination plays another important role. In the beginning of *TMS* Smith says that sympathy is a general principle of "fellow-understanding" that enables me to understand another's passions and interests even if I resent or even abhor those passions or that person. Imagination is important in this scheme, perhaps more important than Smith admits, because it allows one to project oneself and understand what another is feeling even when one is revolted by that feeling. I might, then, understand how someone like Ivan Boesky felt when he was engaged in insider trading, even though I may disapprove of the object of his feelings and passions.

Like his teacher David Hume, Smith breaks with a rationalist tradition by linking moral judgment to moral sentiment. According to Smith, sympathy and imagination are necessary for moral judgment because in judging intentions or actions one must first understand what another feels, or, in the case of oneself, engage in imaginative self-evaluation of one's own emotions that accompany the intention, or action. From this understanding one has a series of second-order emotions deriving from sympathy. Smith calls these moral sentiments of agreement, approval, or disapproval of the intention, activity, and its accompanying emotion. Having understood the sentiments of another, I then determine whether those sentiments agree with my own and approve or disapprove on the basis of societally espoused moral rules, that is, what most agree *ought* to be the case. Finally, I determine what and who will benefit or be harmed by the character or action in question.

Moral judgments are not purely subjective personal reactions, however. Sympathy and imagination are the basis of Smith's impartial spectator theory, which, in turn, accounts for the social nature of moral rules and moral judgments. Sympathy, along with imagination, allows us to disengage ourselves and evaluate a situation or person more dispassionately, judiciously, or impartially. The spectator is that element of human judgment within us that steps back from particular situations to evaluate in terms of a general socially espoused moral rule. Alternatively, in one's mode as an impartial spectator, one may also revise a particular rule to fit a new kind of situation more appropriately. The impartial spectator phenomenon explains how we can not merely understand, judge, approve, or disapprove of one another and our activities but also decide whether a certain character, person, intention, or action is one we *ought* to approve. The basis for the "ought" is what I and others judge, in these impartial moments, to be right or correct. These judgments, both my own and those of others in society, form the basis of moral rules that impartial people would adopt as normative measures of human behavior. Moral rules, in turn, become the basis for impartial moral judgments. According to Smith, moral rules are not predetermined principles written in stone. Rather, they develop out of, are used to evaluate, and are altered because of particular judgments of particular situations. The impartial spectator also is the source of one's own conscience, the element within us able to disengage from oneself, in order to engage in critical self-evaluation, self-criticism, or approval. The impartial spectator within explains our sense of duty, our desire to do what is honorable, noble, and morally correct (Smith, 1759/1976, III.3.4; Werhane, 1991a).

Smith's impartial spectator is an early version of the idea of the moral thin self I developed in chapter 2. Smith's spectator is embedded in a web of social relationships out of which he or she develops the realization that one is more than those relationships. The impartial spectator is the thin self stepping back to evaluate and critique oneself and others and then developing or reiterating moral rules that apply to a social and personal situation.

According to Smith, no one is ever a totally disengaged, completely disinterested, ideal spectator. Rather, Smith's idea of an impartial spectator is that element within each of us, functioning on an individual and social level, that accounts for our ability to distinguish what we do, what we approve of, and what we judge we ought to do and approve of—the social ideals any individual or society sets for itself. Smith's idea adds to my discussion in chapter 2 because it introduces the role of imagination. Functioning adequately as a judicious spectator depends on imagination, moral imagination, to make the interconnections between human character and action, and between sentiments, moral rules, and moral judgments. As a spectator one goes back and forth between a particular situation and its context, between one's moral sentiments and those of others, and then applies general moral rules to evaluate that situation or character. Never does Smith suggest that an impartial spectator merely generates abstract moral rules outside a social context or simply applies the rules without first beginning with the particular—the situational context out of which moral sensibilities and moral judgments arise. Moreover, sometimes, to fit a new kind of situation, this process calls for a reform of general moral rules that depends on an imaginative projection of what individuals agree *should* be approved.

Smith's analysis is prescient, because it forms the basis for much of the contemporary discussion of moral imagination as the ability to empathize, to understand another point of view, and to be creative in ethical decision-making. Moral imagination, along with sympathy, shapes our moral judgments as we impartial spectators discern what society ought to approve, affirming community rather than individual values. Smith does not think that moral judgments are merely a result of general or universal principles that one applies, ad hoc, to all human situations. Rather, he believes moral judgments to result from interactions between persons, situations, and general, revisable rules. This interest in the particular as well as the general in morality and moral judgments, one will recall from earlier discussions, continues later in moral psychologists (e.g., Rest, 1988) and by writers such as Nussbaum, who use literature as a catalyst for development of moral imagination (Nussbaum, 1990, 338–46).

But Smith's work is limited by his assumption that each of us deals with the world in much the same way—through the conceptual scheme of an eighteenth-century Scottish gentleman. Assuming that human nature is homogeneous, one can more easily project and sympathize with another person, or make self-evaluations, and often actually be correct. But, as I argued in chapter 3, each of us functions from a set of mental models, schemas of which most of us are only vaguely aware, not identical even in Scotland, or even among Scottish gentlemen of the same generation. Smith's analysis introduces the idea of moral imagination, but it does not describe how one sympathizes with non-Scots, or account for how we reshape our own mental models and moral rules.

The late-eighteenth-century German philosopher Immanuel Kant further develops the concept of imagination. Kant is credited with the idea that all our sensations are structured through conceptual categories of the understanding that originate in the mind of the perceiver but are universally the same in the minds of each of us. Kant claims that imagination is essential for organizing one's sensations into perceptions, which become representations of experience from which we derive knowledge. Kant distinguishes at least three kinds of imagination: reproductive, productive, and reflective, or free play. What they are and how they are related are subject to some interpretation, but, relying on the work of Rudolf Makkreel, one can summarize these concepts. Because the data of our experiences are nonrecurring, but similar, sensations, one has to account for the fact that we perceive recurring objects, not sense data. Kant argues that the reproductive imagination synthesizes nonrecurring sensations into representations in order to make perception and memory possible. Without reproductive imagination, according to Kant, we would merely be aware of nonrecurring sensations. The reproductive imagination works in at least three ways: (1) it forms images or representations from collections of sensations, (2) it connects these representations to reproduce those images in memory, and (3) it connects images with other similar images, thus enabling recognition (Makkreel, 1990, chapter 1; Werhane, 1984, 192–4).

The productive imagination is more active and has at least three functions. First, it structures, schematizes, and provides order to representations through the categories of understanding so that experience is possible. Its function, then, is "to construe things sensibly present as instantiating pure concepts of the understanding" (Young, 1988, 155). Second, it helps us to make sense out of the categories as pure categories of the understanding, so that, for example, we can think about the category "quantity" abstractly without having to recall a concrete representation of quantitative sensible things (Woods, 1983, 201–5). Third, it synthesizes all our experiences as "ours" from the locus of what Kant calls the "transcendental unity of apperception," the independent nonempirical self, the "I" that is the subject and unity of all that we call "my experiences."

In *Critique of Judgment* (1790/1987) Kant extends his concept of imagination, arguing that in addition to its reproductive and productive functions, imagination engages in free reflection or free play. The imagination in this role, Kant argues, uses material from experience, but "in this process we feel our freedom from the law of association. . . . [A]lthough it is under that law that nature lends us material, yet we can process that material into something quite different, namely into something that surpasses nature" (§182). Representations created by the imagination are aesthetical rather than rational ideas, because they "play" with what we know from experience and also sometimes manipulate the categories of understanding. For example, we can create unicorns, images of gods, stories, myths, fantasies, and music, all of which play with experience. We can also imagine four-dimensional space, geometries in multidimensions, and mathematical number systems, and play with the logic of those systems without their experiential ground.

Aesthetical ideas go beyond reason, according to Kant; they have no adequate counterparts in actual experience or in the categories of the understanding. Thus, they are creative associations, both in content (how they manipulate experience) and form (how they manipulate universal categories of the understanding). According to Rudolf Makkreel, "[a]esthetic ideas add to our interpretation of experience by suggesting significant affinities even when direct conceptual connections are lacking" (1990, 5). Imagination in this third sense, as free reflection, is then neither mimetic nor rationally productive. It does not merely re-present our sensations as perceptions or experience; neither does it just mimic or represent experience. It is not restricted to working within the categories of the understanding or the confines of reason as Kant defines those terms. Indeed, Kant calls the aesthetical idea an "inexponible presentation" (1790/1987, §343).

Kant claims that

> an aesthetical idea is a presentation of the imagination which is conjoined with a given concept, and is connected, when we use imagination in its freedom, with such a multiplicity of partial presentations that no expression that stands for a determinate concept can be found for it. Hence it is a presentation that makes us add to a concept the thoughts of which that is ineffable. (1790/1987 §316)

Aesthetical ideas are often the creative ideas of geniuses, and thus the source of great art. Because they are creations of the imagination rather than reason, aesthetical ideas and their counterpart representations in works of art can be appreciated as ideas apart from, and indeed at a distance from, their purpose, function, representational accuracy, or utility, as purely contemplative aesthetic objects.

Nevertheless, free reflection begins with and uses perceptions, experience, memories, and concepts of the understanding as its material. It is not to be identified with the transcendental self in the act of creation. (See, for example, Coleridge, 1907/1973, 21.) Kant simply does not make that sort of connection between free reflective imagination and the transcendental unity of apperception, and it will be important for my purposes that he did not.

Kant does not elaborate on an idea of *moral* imagination, and, given the role of rationality in his moral theory, this is not surprising. Makkreel points out that according to Kant, one can consider the intellectual beauty of the construction of moral laws, just as one can consider the beauty of a painting. We can appreciate formulations of the categorical imperative and admire the ideal of their purposiveness disengaged from actual purposiveness in practical reason and morality (Makkreel, 1990, 125–7). But this is different from linking imagination directly to morality. In *Critique of Practical Reason* Kant (1789/1983) claims that the productive imagination (the second form of imagination according to my reading of Kant) cannot function in moral judgment because moral judgments entail the categorical imperative, the form of all moral laws that directs the transcendental subject; thus, the categorical imperative is not experienced, and, unlike aesthetic objects, is exempt from schematization by the categories of the understanding (Johnson, 1993, 70–2).

Mark Johnson contends, however, that the idea of moral imagination derives from Kant's concepts of natural law and free reflection. Kant's use of the term "law of nature" or "universal law of nature" in the first formulation of the categorical imperative ("Act as though the maxim of your action were by your will to be a universal law of nature," (Kant, 1784/1959; f421) is a metaphorical bridge, so that Kant's universal law of nature is the practical analog of the categorical imperative. Moral judgment, then, "involves an act of imaginative envisionment of a nonexisting world (the kingdom of ends) as a means for judging a proposed maxim" (Johnson, 1985, 273). This metaphorical dimension or imaginative envisionment is very much like Kant's description of free reflection in *Critique of Judgment* where the imagination makes reflective judgments about *possible* representations or concepts. More simply put, moral imagination might have a role in Kant's moral theory as "the ability to envision the pattern of human life and action which is embedded in one's decisions and actions" (Rossi, 1980, 157), or as the ability to envision how my decisions and actions embody, or fail to embody, Kant's ideal of the categorical imperative functioning in an ideal kingdom of ends.

Kant's analysis is helpful in sorting out various forms of imagination, and he initiates the idea that imagination is not merely mimetic. But if Kant views moral imagination at all, it is most likely as an aesthetical idea, not as part of the practice of acting in accordance to various formulations of the categorical imperative. Moreover, even if Johnson and Rossi are correct in their interpretations, there is still a difficulty. We are left with Kant's assumption that ideally there is one universal moral law and a unified notion of the kingdom of ends. Those are the ideals of morality, the models to which all moral action and moral judgment should aspire. But if the arguments of chapter 3 are correct, there could be other models in which another form of moral principle is embedded (e.g., the principle of utility) that is considered to be universal, and adopting that principle might create different grounds for moral judgments than adopting the categorical imperative.

MORAL IMAGINATION

Given the thinking of Smith and Kant, I now turn to a more finely tuned definition of moral imagination. Mark Johnson describes moral imagination as

> [1] self-knowledge about the imaginative structure of our moral understanding, including its values, limitations, and blind spots . . . [2] similar knowledge of other people . . . [3] [the ability to] imagine how various actions open to us might alter our self-identity, modify our commitments, change our relationships, and affect the lives of others. . . [4] what it might mean, in terms of possibilities for enhanced meaning and relationships, for us to perform this or that action . . . [and 5] the ability to imagine and to enact transformations in our moral understanding, our character, and our behavior. (1993, 187)

The term "imaginatively" refers to what Johnson in another place calls "metaphoric understanding, [the] projective process in which we structure one domain by means of principles and material taken from a different kind of domain" (1985, 274–5). He also refers to moral imagination as *"imaginative rationality* that is at once insightful, critical, exploratory, and transformative" (1993, 202).

I define the "projective process" as the ability to understand the nature of a conceptual scheme and mental models; the ability to distinguish various "structure[s] of our moral understanding," assuming that different mental models structure moral understanding differently; and the capacity to envision their implications in present and fresh contexts. This process is imaginative just because, given a nexus of mental models, one envisions them and how they affect one's interpretation of the situation. Given that, as Senge claims, mental models ordinarily "exist below the level of awareness" (1990, 176), the process is also imaginative only if one distinguishes the operative or dominating script at hand; grasps its strengths, incompleteness, and its shortcomings; and envisions other applicable points of view or scripts that could similarly define, and apply to, this particular context.

Johnson ties his notion of moral imagination to his theory of metaphor. This leads him to conclude that

> [m]oral reasoning is a constructive imaginative activity. . . . Our most fundamental moral concepts (e.g., will, freedom, law, right, duty, well-being, action) are defined metaphorically, typically by multiple metaphoric mappings for a single concept. The way we conceptualize a particular situation will depend on our use of systematic conceptual metaphors that make up the common understanding of members of our culture. (1993, 2)

I agree that "the way we conceptualize . . . will depend on our use of . . . conceptual metaphors." But I argued in chapter 3 that these metaphors, which I labeled conceptual schemes and mental models, are neither thoroughly systemic nor simply common cultural understandings. They are much more complex, partly idiosyncratic, partly ethnically, religiously, culturally, socially, and historically based. Each of us functions through a bundle of mental models that overlap with each other and with each other's schema. These schema are partly, but not wholly, governed by "common cultural understanding" that includes a shared language or languages. Some of them are idiosyncratic; others broader, more universal in range and scope. Underlying is a common coordinate system that accounts for cross-schematic or cross-cultural understanding, evaluation, and revision of metaphors. "Our most fundamental moral concepts . . . are defined metaphorically," but in the sense that each is embedded in a conceptual scheme and a set of mental models that frame and shape its meaning. Moreover, each is incomplete and revisable. However, as I argued in chapter 3 and shall reinforce in chapter 6, the universality of conceptual schemes and mental models or conceptual metaphors and the fact that all experience is constituted by a conceptual scheme do not result in obvious relativist implications.

Johnson is not altogether clear about the distinction between *moral* imagination and other forms of free reflection. I propose that moral imagination, unlike some other forms of free reflection, begins not with the general but with the particular, a particular person of moral or immoral character, an event, a situation, a dilemma, or a conflict. Second, moral imagination entails the ability to disengage. Third, *moral* imagination, as distinct from free reflection, deals not merely with fantasies but with possibilities or ideals that, if not practical, are at least theoretically viable and actualizable. Further, these possibilities have a normative or prescriptive character; they concern what one *ought* to do, with right or wrong, with virtue, with positive or negative consequences, or with what common morality calls "good" or "evil." This activity is imaginative when it explores a wide range of possibilities not merely explicit in the circumstance in question, or, on the other hand, fully explicated by moral abstractions such as the categorical imperative or the principle of utility.

Kant's concepts of productive imagination and free reflection are useful in thinking about another dimension of moral imagination. Moral imagination, if effective, not only fantasizes creatively about fresh options or new possibilities from a normative perspective. Merck's researchers and managers could think creatively about developing Mectizan because they were not trapped in only one perspective. From a neo-Kantian perspective, their productive imaginations understood the schema or "concepts of the understanding" ordinarily at work at Merck (e.g., that Merck developed only drugs that had a consumer base of $20 million per year). They also were familiar with George Merck's dictum that medicine is for the people, a slogan at Merck. Thus, Merck's researchers and managers were able to find another perspective on the "normal managerial script" that governs much of management decision-making and choice of research direction. Part of the job of moral imagination is to perceive the ethical dimensions of a managerial or corporate situation. Further, moral imagination helps us disengage from situational or organizational perspectives and consider viable alternative possibilities based on reasonable moral standards. Vagolos's appeal to George Merck's statement gave him good reasons to approve research on Mectizan, "ammunition" to back up his decision, even though his reasons were not those commonly used to evaluate research projects at for-profit organizations.

In clarifying moral imagination, John Kekes, in "Moral Imagination, Freedom, and the Humanities" (1991) and in *The Morality of Pluralism* (1993),distinguishes four kinds of imagination: imaging, problem-solving, fantasizing, and moral imagination, "the mental exploration of what it would be like to realize particular possibilities" (Kekes, 1991, 101) and "evaluating the possibilities . . . as good or evil" (Kekes, 1993, 101). Kekes claims that moral imagination has two aspects. Moral imagination is, first, the threefold imaginative re-creation of possibilities [including] those that were generally *available* in the agents' context, those that the agents could reasonably have been *expected* to believe themselves to have, and those that the agents *actually* believed themselves to have" (Kekes, 1991, 102, my emphasis). Moral imagination also includes a second element, the evaluation of these possibilities in terms of their moral worth, a process both exploratory and corrective. According to Kekes, one of the ways to develop moral imagination, that is, to expand the scope of one's beliefs and thus one's possibilities from the point of view of what a "reasonable agent" would do, is to engage in retrospection. This process, Kekes contends, gives one a better understanding of how one's belief structure operates and helps one to redirect that belief structure in the future.

Let us see how that might work in the case of the *Challenger* explosion. According to his own retrospection, Roger Boisjoly, the developer of the O-rings, was aware that his belief structure was restricted by the Thiokol script even before the explosion. At the same time, as early as the seventh shuttle launch, Boisjoly was aware of this script and its effect on his belief structure. While outsiders might argue that Boisjoly could reasonably have been expected to blow the whistle to top management at Morton before the launch, given the culture and operative scripts at Thiokol at that time, under those conditions, Boisjoly was unable to process that alternative even though he thought he was being manipulated by Thiokol's managers (Boisjoly, 1988, 17–22). Kekes claims that merely being aware of possibilities is not itself imaginative. I disagree, using as evidenced the Boisjoly scenario. That case suggests that one condition for being morally imaginative is awareness of one's situation and recognition of possibilities beyond those seemingly prescribed or proscribed by one's context or role. There was imaginative thinking in Boisjoly's early recognition that he had been locked into a point of view that precluded exploring new possibilities. At the same time, Boisjoly could not change the operative Thiokol script affecting his own decision-making. So merely attacking a dilemma from what Kekes calls the perspective of a "reasonable agent" is not enough, always, to trigger envisioning new possibilities, even those that appear to be available to the agent. Boisjoly was a reasonable agent, so was Dennis Gioia. Yet they were trapped in a positionally objective point of view. Everything made sense and was reasonable from that positional perspective. Boisjoly was imaginative enough to see problems beforehand and realize the limits of his situation and Thiokol's operative mental model. But he was unable to go beyond this awareness, and thus his moral imagination was incomplete.

What, then, is moral imagination? Moral imagination begins with a particular case, scenario, or event in which we become engaged as thick social selves. In the particular, our moral sentiments begin to function, in Smith's sense, to understand the anguish and complexity in the dilemma at hand. Most important, one begins with the particular because ethical issues arise in specific real-life situations, not in abstract moral theory, although moral theory is about particular events. Simply considering principles such as the categorical imperative or the principle of utility divorced from a particular case or example interests philosophers working on metaethics. But such abstract analyses, if separated from examples, are not as relevant in applied ethics. Moreover, merely applying general principles to particular situations often creates a disconnect between moral theories and moral dilemmas, as I argued in chapter 2, and as the Nestlé and Lockheed cases illustrate. Recall that in the Lockheed case, in which the CEO faced paying extortion to receive a much needed airplane contract, a utilitarian perspective might have sanctioned paying the extortion; a deontological perspective would not. Nestlé's marketing of infant formula in developing African countries illustrated that general principles, in this case, marketing strategies, do not work in the same ways in different contexts. So beginning with the particular grounds the moral conflict or dilemma.

Beginning with awareness of the particular, moral imagination, functioning analogously to Kant's notion of the reproductive imagination, includes (1) awareness of the character, context, situation, event, and dilemma at issue; (2) awareness of the script or schema function in that context and role relationships entailed in that context, and (3) awareness of possible moral conflicts or dilemmas that might arise in that situation, including dilemmas created at least in part by the dominating script or the situation itself.

However, the human mind seldom rests on the particular, so moral imagination entails a second factor, the productive imagination. Almost all of us always generalize from a particular case to other similar and dissimilar characters, situations, or experiences. The productive *moral* imagination is critical as we generalize, because one could argue that bond traders such as Paul Mozer or Joseph Jett at Kidder were highly imaginative. They connected their trading to what they perceived to be the operative script at Salomon and Kidder, or what they deemed the script should be, creating very imaginative trading schemes. Apparently they did not challenge and evaluate their activities from any other *moral* perspective, such as the perspective of common morality (assuming that in their personal lives they were decent people, as all evidence about these men indicates). Because they did not challenge the framing script or schema operative at Salomon and Kidder, or at least the script they *thought* should be defining their activities and expectations, their activities became morally questionable. Mired in a particular context with a dominant operating script, one must confront and question the script to challenge one's perspective on an activity (e.g., that exceeding legal limits of Treasury purchases, trading in customers' accounts without their knowledge or permission, or phantom trading may be unethical, not to mention illegal). This awareness of an incomplete, perhaps even limiting or distorting script and one's subsequent challenge to it require what Kant would call a productive moral imagination.

Roger Boisjoly, unlike Mozer and Jett, debated the dilemmas over his professional expertise and moral requirements as an engineer and the constraints of NASA and Thiokol. Unlike Jett and Mozer, Boisjoly was clear about what the right decision should be: that the *Challenger* should not have been launched on January 28. He knew the limitations of the NASA and Thiokol mental models. Thus, Boisjoly had a highly productive moral imagination. But he could not make the further extrapolation; he was unable to circumvent the corporate culture and the implicit idea that engineers are just that—engineers—who defer to management for the final decisions.

Interestingly, the J&J Tylenol incidents illustrate how a dominant script can become a positive driving force for moral imagination. In permanently pulling the capsules off the market, James Burke and other managers at J&J broke with a number of commonly held management practices. They violated precepts of good marketing practice; they questioned their legal counsel, who was afraid this action would be perceived as an admission of guilt; and they placed their customers first as their primary stakeholders, even superseding their commitment to their shareholders to continue as a very profitable company. Yet the decision to eliminate Tylenol capsules was not a revelation that transformed that company. Rather, there was a corporate culture at J&J, prompted by their credo, that lent credence to this decision. Later some managers at J&J and Burke himself said that given the credo they had no choice—it was a "no brainer." According to the credo, customers were simply first priority, and given that principle, the decision was "natural" (Smith and Tedlow, 1989).

The productive moral imagination is usually triggered by the impartial spectator, the thin self in its critical mode. This element of moral imagination is essential to become aware of one's social roles and role relationships and to evaluate the demands and limits of role morality. The managers at MiniScribe were very creative, but only in their roles as MiniScribe managers whose primary overriding duty was to the survival of the company. Thus, most of them did not step back to evaluate the absurdity of their actions for the long-term viability of MiniScribe.

Moral imagination entails a third element, analogous to, but not exactly identical with, what Kant called free reflection. Being imaginative entails not merely awareness of a moral conflict but also awareness of a different mental model. In the *Challenger* case, on the night before the launch neither the engineers nor the managers at Thiokol were able to critique the conceptual schemes in which they were operating, a great deal to expect from any person in that stressful situation. But it illustrates how building certain habits can create a script that is very difficult to evaluate or escape from, even when doing so might, in retrospect, have changed the outcome. Creative moral imagination or free reflection, when operative, helps us to project beyond the constraints of particular scripts or biases. Creative imagination facilitates the ability to envision and actualize novel, morally justifiable possibilities through a fresh point of view or conceptual scheme. Thus, creative moral imagination helps us criticize our own and others' points of view, and generate adequate alternatives.

That one can change the script or operative mental model is illustrated in the Merck case. Merck challenged the "tradition" of using profitability as the basis for choosing research projects. It sponsored the development, manufacture, and distribution of a drug that likely will never even repay the cost of its development. It placed curing disease and the integrity of its researchers ahead of its own criteria of profitability and shareholder returns, criteria that had sometimes dictated restricting drug development to products foreseeably producing a revenue of $20 million per year.

What is distinctive about *moral* imagination in all these examples is that at each stage of decision-making the imagination enables critiquing the situation at hand and evaluation of newly formulated possibilities and justification of possibilities outside a given script or a defined role, such as giving away a drug or pulling a popular product off the market. The moral imagination resembles Smith's imaginative spectator, moving one's thinking from the status quo to new possibilities and then evaluating those possibilities by some norm, perhaps a company credo or statement of principle, or other more general principles of morality.

In this evaluative facilitation, moral imagination may play another role, that of enabling creative thinking about how to revise or revamp common precepts of morality set forth by a particular group, religious community, culture, or society behavior norms. Revising moral rules or moral standards may seem extreme, but I can give an obvious and very simple example. Given newly developed awareness of environmental degradation in the late twentieth century, we are now in the process of revising our theory of human rights to include the right to a viable environment and rights of future generations as part of common morality. We can then use these revised moral rules in criticizing individual, organizational, institutional, and societal habits of consumption, pollution, and waste. From particular evidence of environmental degradation and the limits of the ecosystem, we are altering our moral precepts, thus moving from the particular to the general, and then using revised moral standards or rules to evaluate specific environmental practices.

To illustrate,

> [t]wenty years ago, the typical American paper mill spewed 40 million gallons of contaminated water a day into a nearby river or stream and belched fumes that stank like rotten eggs and corroded the metal of cars for miles around.
>
> Today, the Weyerhaeuser Company's mill in [Oglethorpe] Georgia releases just 11 million gallons of much cleaner effluent a day into the Flint River and emits a faint and not unpleasant scent resembling turpentine. And many other paper producers . . . are following the same pristine path. (Holusha, 1996, A35)

Twenty years ago it was commonly assumed pollution and waste were inevitable byproducts of operating pulp and paper mills. Paper mills commonly discharged millions of gallons of polluted water and disgorged unpleasant polluting discharges into the air. The waste generated was thought of as just that—unusable garbage that had to be disposed of. The standard argument at that time was that this pollution was an inherent part of producing paper. To change these processes would be inordinately expensive, and indeed, some argued, virtually impossible technologically. Recycling paper was too costly, and recycled paper products were not acceptable to most consumers.

Today, the leading mills such as those owned by Weyerhaeuser, Champion International, and Louisiana Pacific, have revamped their processes, cutting pollution by up to 80%, developing new processes for recycling paper that are inexpensive and produce decent paper, and recovering for reuse chemicals formerly dumped into local streams. Technology has been developed that is cost effective, and pulp mills are becoming increasingly sound environmentally, and ecologically conservative. This is a revolution—a revolution not just in production but in thinking about production—a revolution in the mental model of pulp manufacture. This revolution is due, in part, to increased regulations on the industry. But it is also due to an imaginative realization that conservation saves money, that there are new profitable uses for what was once called waste, and that it is to the competitive advantage of pulp producers to respond, as customers become more demanding for "green" processes and products. It took great imagination to disengage a well-entrenched and profitable industry from the mental model mandating inevitable pollution and useless wastes. And it took *moral* imagination to develop critical self-evaluation of these traditional practices. Pulp manufacturers have learned, for example, that

> [r]ecycling has economic payoffs beyond just potential savings on water costs. For example, many mills have developed the technology for recovering and reusing the chemicals that separate the cellulose fibers in wood that are transformed into paper from the lignin glue that holds a tree together. . . . [According to one plant manager,] "We simply could not afford to run the plant unless we could recover the digesting chemicals." (Holusha, 1996, A37)

In 1975, no one could have imagined a pulp manufacturer uttering those words.

We see in this illustration a particular environmental problem with pulp manufacture coupled with increasingly alarming evidence of environmental degradation. Environmental regulation and a revision of environmental moral standards have resulted. Because of all these factors, pulp mills have transformed those regulations and standards into particular solutions that are advantageous to paper manufacture and to the environment and to creation of new technologies that become competitively transforming as well.

CONCLUSION

Moral imagination is both creative and applied. As reproductive imagination, it enables us to become aware of the moral demands of particular events and the conceptual schemes or mental models operating in specific contexts. As productive imagination, moral imagination accounts for our ability to reframe our experiences in different terms, so that we can evaluate our operative mental models and critique role demands. As free reflection, moral imagination helps in developing fresh interpretations of particular scenarios and creating new perspectives. But moral imagination is not merely creative or exploratory. Moral imagination enables us to integrate common morality into decision processes and moral judgments, anticipate untoward consequences, and project new practical solutions that take into account a variety of points of view and respond to or even create moral demands. Finally, moral imagination accounts for the possibility of interaction between similar cases, new data, and moral rules, so that we can rethink traditional solutions to similar problems and revise the moral rules that justify evaluative judgments. Moral imagination thus is an enabling mechanism for the ongoing process of moral deliberation and moral judgment that is not merely reactive, sentimental, or absolutist.

Have I asked too much of moral imagination? Is it doing all the work of, or displacing, moral reasoning? Is there not a role for the impartial, reasonable spectator as well as the imaginative one? Is there only a minor role for moral principles? In the next chapter I address these questions.

6

Moral Reasoning and Moral Imagination

The South Shore Bank is located on the South Side of Chicago in an area covering a neighborhood population of about 80,000. Before the 1960s the neighborhood consisted of lower-middle-class and middle-class apartments and houses and one four-block-square section of mansions. The neighborhood was primarily Jewish, and there was a tradition of staying in the neighborhood, then moving to more affluent areas as one's economic status improved. In the 1960s there was a mass migration of blacks into the Northern cities and a subsequent "white flight" from certain city neighborhoods, including South Shore. By 1970 the population of South Shore was primarily black and poor, and it was predicted that within five years the neighborhood would become one of the worst slums in Chicago. The South Shore Bank, whose deposits had steadily fallen to $42 million, was for sale. Because it was the last financial institution in that neighborhood, regulatory statutes at that time prohibited closing or moving the bank. Given the socioeconomic prospects of this neighborhood and its obvious financial precariousness, no financial institution in the Chicago area (or indeed anywhere) was willing to purchase the South Shore Bank or invest in this area. From a dispassionate perspective, from any reasonable point of view, investing in South Shore was irrational and ill-conceived.

Despite advice to the contrary, in 1973 a group of entrepreneurs, led by Ronald Grzywinski, borrowed enough money to buy the South Shore Bank for under $4 million. Today, still located in South Shore, this bank has assets of over $200 million; it is profitable, although not wildly so; and its net loan losses in 1995 were .48%, one of lowest for any bank of its size. Yet, until recently, most of its loans were to the South Shore neighborhood. (Recently it started a branch in a second low-income neighborhood in Chicago, the Austin neighborhood, and it has also opened a bank and developed a lending program in rural Arkansas.)

The bank focused its attention on housing, lending money to small contractors and individuals willing to restore buildings in South Shore. It also set up a series of subsidiaries. One concentrates on real estate development, another on minority business enterprises. Another, a nonprofit institution, works with state and federal programs to restore and develop housing for low-income residences, and one serves as a consulting firm for these other projects. It has raised money through what it calls development deposits, encouraging wealthy people from other neighborhoods to open accounts at South Shore. Today South Shore, still over 70% black except in the mansion area, which is an integrated neighborhood, is a viable place to live. The South Shore Bank has been directly responsible for funding over one third of the residential restorations and has lent money to neighborhood businesses as well. Drugs and gangs are virtually absent, and more than three fourths of the residences and apartments are in good condition.

South Shore Bank linked traditional expertise in lending to viable customers with the social aim or rehabilitating the South Shore neighborhood. Yet the bank's social goals were also economic, because the bank could not have survived if the neighborhood had remained in its deleterious 1973 state. To get and retain customers, the bank had to provide a neighborhood where customers could feel comfortable. So improving the neighborhood was necessary for the bank's success and was also an important social contribution.

South Shore Bank lent and still lends money to contractors and individuals of good character with solid reputations for honesty, job security, and good debt payment rather than only to people who have measurable monetary net worth. As a result, many of their clients are people who could not obtain loans at the larger Chicago banks yet are low-risk borrowers.

Interestingly, South Shore Bank officers do not claim to be Mother Teresas. Rather, they argue, they lend money to people and enterprises that are less risky than many recipients of Big Bank loans, such as developing countries whose ability to repay has not always equaled that of the individuals to whom South Shore built its customer base. Today South Shore Bank and its holding company, Shorebank Corporation, are models for community development financial institutions (Esty, 1995; Grzywinski, 1991; McMillen, Powell, and Werhane, 1998; Remey and Dees, 1993; Taub, 1988).

Some critics of South Shore Bank have argued, correctly, that Grzywinski could have taken the original investment and made much more money and that South Shore Bank has not adequately maximized returns on its investments and assets (Esty, 1995). Because it does not provide competitive earnings for its investors, it is, in fact, subsidized by these investments. Yet, according to South Shore Bank officers, the "payoff" is not merely profits, but also the resurrection of a dead and abandoned neighborhood. Thus, it has returned to its investors and shareholders what the bank had promised in the first place.

In chapter 5 I argued that moral imagination is essential for creative moral decision-making that was not merely contextual, role-driven, or institutionally constrained. In this chapter I want to link moral imagination and moral judgment to a limited notion of moral objectivity in the following arguments.

- Moral imagination is a necessary but not a sufficient condition for moral decision-making.
- The contention that "moral understanding is *fundamentally* imaginative in character" (Johnson, 1993, 217) is a questionable thesis. Without moral imagination one can remain mired in a particular situation or within a particular mental model; without moral reasoning one may slip into moral fantasy.
- A particular moral judgment derives from "a specific kind of reflective, exploratory, and critical process of evaluation carried out through communal discourse and practice" (Johnson, 1993, 217). But moral judgments are not merely a result of communal discourse and practice. They depend on, and form the basis of, moral rules and moral standards that are not merely traditionally, culturally, or communally grounded, and moral judgments appeal to standards that do not merely arise from, or depend on, communal discourse.

Given that all experience is conceptually framed, *"moral objectivity consists, not in having an absolute 'God's-eye point of view'"* (Johnson, 1993, 217, emphasis Johnson's). Nevertheless, I shall question Mark Johnson's thesis that "moral reasoning is a constructive imaginative activity that is based, not primarily on universal moral laws, but principally on metaphoric concepts"(1993, 2). I shall argue instead that:

- The concept of moral imagination, by itself, does not entail bringing into question all forms of moral objectivity, particularly the view that moral objectivity is an (albeit unreachable) goal and the ground of moral decision-making and moral judgment. Therefore,
- One can make a case for limited moral objectivity that does not rely on an "absolute 'God's-eye point of view.'"

A DISENGAGED VIEW FROM SOMEWHERE

As I argued in chapter 5, moral imagination enables each of us to develop discourse between the particular (a particular case or event) and the general, between "communal discourse and practice" and a less engaged, more "critical process of evaluation," or "between fine-tuned perception of particulars and a rule-governed concern for general obligations" (Nussbaum, 1990, 157). Moral imagination enables the development of a critical, thin, spectator self. Without moral imagination one has difficulty distancing oneself from mental models operative in a particular context. In those instances one often fails to evaluate that conceptual scheme, its limiting perspective, and the consequences it produces, from another point of view. On the other hand, as demonstrated in chapter 4, an overpreoccupation with imagination, coupled with a simplistic narrative approach, may lead to distortions or even creations of fact, as we saw in reports of the Pinto and Salomon Brothers cases. The internalization or acceptance of a particular narrative account may result in discounting scientifically verified (positionally objective) data, or, alternately, treating emotional reactions as irrational, as illustrated in positions on the Dow-Corning breast implant controversies. Merely stimulating one's imagination may lead one to accept an interpretation of a series of events, such as the Audi acceleration case shown on *60 Minutes,* just because it is creative and plausible. Or imagination may create a set of explanatory narratives that, while coherent and reasonable, tell stories that may or may not describe actual events, as the Salomon Brothers/Paul Mozer stories illustrate. Imagination, alone, then, as free play, can create fantasies or justify a parochial set of values consistent with a particular narrative just because it is imaginative and creative.

The narrative story in which an event or a person is a part contributes to the event and cannot be ignored. Nevertheless, merely recounting narratives may not allow one to perceive the relevant operative mental models and thus reinforces the problem and accounts, in part, for its iteration. For example, if one begins with the thesis that the odds for space shuttle explosions are very low, this thesis or frame becomes part of space shuttle narratives, reinforcing a questionable approach to risk evaluation and encouraging of optimism that can preclude more appropriate analyses of risk. Only when one reformulates that thesis in different terms can a narrative be altered so that new perspectives on space travel risk emerge. Similarly, if one's imagination creates a causal connection between illnesses and breast implants, and if one has an implant and is ill, it is difficult to accept other explanations, and that connection becomes the explicatory frame for the stories women with implants tell about their illnesses. Being moral imaginative involves challenging very basic assumptions, for example, interpreting correlations as cause-and-effect relationships. At the same time one has to replace those assumptions with other reasonable, and in some sense corroborated, explanations. To replace the cause-and-effect stories of ill women with implants with a contention that the illnesses are made up or "all in their minds," for example, simply replaces a questionable causal connection with another.

Still, because reality is framed by a conceptual scheme and sets of mental models, apparently each of us lives in a set of narratives created by a scheme or mental model wherein there are only narratives or texts and no possibility for objective challenges, appeals to more general moral principles, or truly impartial moral tests. If all our experiences and thus our reasoning processes and knowledge are embedded in a conceptual scheme, how can we learn how a particular schema functions. How can we evaluate a prototypical interpretation or scripted series of events? How can we be discriminating or imaginative *except* through a conceptual scheme and the set of mental models in which we are imagining, schemes and scripts that control the direction of that discrimination and imagination? Nothing short of a very active free-playing imagination will enable us to distance ourselves from our scripts, roles, or narratives to envision new possible scripts. To be truly imaginative, we must be disengaged, yet even "at a distance" we will be operating within a scheme.

These conceptual constraints, however, are not as regressive or circular as they appear. In the process of analyzing the limits of roles and role obligations, in chapter 2 I argued that one cannot perceive the self except in its roles and other social relationships. Nevertheless, it is necessary to postulate a thin notion of the self as an explanatory mechanism to account for the differences between role obligations and one's moral responsibility for roles and role acts and to explain the phenomena of self-identity and human choice. In chapter 3, I distinguished language, conceptual schemes, narratives, and mental models or scripts from Davidson's "common coordinate system," the bedrock of human activity. There I argued that, just because we are always operating within a scheme or framework, and even if what we call "reality" is always contextualized, does not imply either subjectivism or most forms of conceptual relativism.

Chapter 4 introduced Amartya Sen's positional objectivity, qualifying it to take into account the disparity of conceptual schemes and mental models. There I concluded that position-dependency defines the way in which the object appears "from a delineated somewhere" so that any person in that position sharing the same conceptual scheme (or, on a smaller scale, the same or similar mental model) is able to make similar observations or draw similar conclusions. Sen argues that no position-

ally objective view is complete; almost every position has alternatives
generated either from ignored data or, as I argued, from different ways
of construing the object or event in question. In almost every instance,
other data or alternative ways of framing events are available that one
could adapt to challenge a positionally objective conclusion. I shall argue
further that challenges are possible only when, minimally, one is able to
become at least partially distanced from the view, the data, or situation.
While a "God's-eye point of view" or transpositional view from nowhere
is impossible except as a constructed critique of a particular event or
conceptual scheme, no positionally objective view is merely relative or
immune from challenge, even within the parameters of a particular set
of narratives. Clearly, when there are contradictory narratives or frameworks, there is even more opportunity for raising questions about the
operative mental models. We can now turn that argument into a more
positive analysis of how we can imaginatively disengage from operative
conceptual schemes.

Sen introduces the notion of a "constructed view from nowhere" to
account for our ability to compare various positionally objective points
of view to make coherent sense of them and, in this process, develop
other general theses about what is being observed or experienced. This
is exactly what was at work in Gioia's retrospective self-examination of
his behavior as recall coordinator at Ford and in Boisjoly's pre-and post-
disaster analysis of the *Challenger* shuttle. Such transpositional assessments are crucial when there are clashes of narratives. These assessments, however, depend on a well-developed moral imagination in
order to begin the disengagement and assessment processes.

Transpositional assessments are *constructed* views, because they depend on trans-positional conceptual schemes shared by the assessors.
There are a number of reasons why we can disengage ourselves from
a particular point of view, understand various perspectives, and make
trans-positional assessments. First, we all share a common coordinate
system that grounds our differences. Therefore, there is a common
ground out of which the myriad of mental models develops, accounting
for their overlap. Second, a thin theory of the self, developed in chapter
2, accounts for our ability to understand the limits and incompleteness
of the mental models we employ. Because we are not merely the sum of
our roles, our history, our social relationships, and our practices, we are
at once involved in the nexus of narratives and social relationships that
make up who we are, and at the same time we can function as a critic
and evaluator of those relationships and narratives. Third, no mental
model is complete; hence, we can accommodate fresh ones. Fourth, we
are, or can be, imaginative, morally imaginative. Thus, we can critique
and change our mental models. Transpositional schemes, then, are
shared or shareable, and they too can be questioned on the basis of

their coherence or explanatory scope. These questions, while disengaged from a particular narrative or positional objective point of view, could be asked only from another conceptual scheme or mental model, and revisions of the scheme or schema in question, will, of course produce another schema. Sometimes, however, these assessments and questions are revolutionary, leading to paradigm shifts or dramatic revisions of a conceptual scheme, as Thomas Kuhn argued so well (Kuhn, 1962/1970).

I call these transpositional assessments disengaged views from somewhere rather than constructed views from nowhere. Although they involve disengagement from a particular narrative and set of mental models, they can never entail either complete impartiality or absolute disengagement from some place. They are always grounded in a conceptual scheme and operate from a set of mental models even while challenging those schema.

We may now conclude that none of us is necessarily embedded in a blindly situated, socially constructed perspective so that one cannot be imaginatively reflective, evaluative, and critical. As various cases I have examined suggest, it is critical to disengage from the operating narratives or communal discourses and from the perspectives of colleagues, constituents, personal and professional roles, and from one's organizational, institutional, or regulatory framework. Examining extant narratives is helpful; moral imagination is essential for extrication. For example, as I noted in chapter 1, General Electric (GE) has been cited for more violations of government contracts than any other military contractor, and this is probably not an anomaly. Rather, these occurrences suggest repeated decision-making based on assumptions that have not been adequately challenged or replaced within GE, despite this company's overall success (Hansell, 1994, A1).

How does one distance oneself from one's current operative mental models? How does one become imaginatively reflective and develop a disengaged view from somewhere? Interestingly, Adam Smith is helpful in sorting out a concept of self-reflective impartiality that, coupled with an active imagination, can help to develop habits of creative moral decision-making. Whereas Smith claimed that humans are intrinsically social beings and "can subsist only in society," he also argued that it is possible imaginatively to step back from one's situation within society and view it from another perspective. The impartial spectator, one will remember, explains how we are when we are engaged in acts of evaluation, self-reflection, and moral judgment when we try to step out of a context and take another perspective that is as disengaged, disinterested, or unbiased as possible. This new perspective is neither idealized (a God's-eye view) nor opaque or behind a Rawlsian "veil of ignorance." This is a psychologically distanced view from somewhere that is not disengaged from our personal, historical, cultural, institutional, and social background. In taking such perspective a person tries to disengage from the exigencies of the situation to look at the world and oneself from a more dispassionate point of view, from the point of view of another person, or from the perspective of another narrative or conceptual scheme. In our roles as imaginative impartial spectators, Smith suggests, from a particular character or situation we move to more general moral rules and engage our sympathy in reactive moral sentiments of approval and disapproval. In this way we make moral judgments *about* the particular person, character, situation, or set of events that are not merely *of* the particular, and sometimes we alter the rules in question. But we begin, always, with the particular, and it is because of that starting place that imagination is essential to enable disengagement. Being imaginative and at the same time acting as a disengaged spectator allows one not only to get a critical and evaluative perspective on a script or mental model, but also allows one to be self-reflective: to step back from one's situation and view the event or oneself from another vantage point, but never a view from nowhere.

An impartial spectator theory such as Smith's helps explain how, ordinarily, each of us is a product of and engaged in a set of communities and narratives linked by imaginative sympathy, mutual interests, and interdependence. Still, the phenomenon of the core thin self enables us to act as spectators and critics of the very mental models in which we are engaged. Thus, we are able to step back from our engagements to become a critic and initiator of change.

Additionally, my analysis of moral imagination in the preceding chapter provides an outline for moral imaginative judgment that at least implicitly includes a role for a reasonable, impartial, or judicious spectator. In every aspect of moral imagination, reasonable limited impartiality plays a role. Accompanying creative moral imagination, then, are three control elements: a disengaged view from somewhere, reasonability, and appeals to common morality. Reproductive imagination, entailing the process of disengagement and discernment of moral dilemmas and the operative framing scripts, is both imaginative, and, in discernment, at least not irrational. For even in this mode one is comparing one set of scenarios to others and evaluating what is at stake. Productive imagination challenges and often reformulates the event and its script in different terms. As free reflection, moral imagination is not spontaneous or unbridled free play. It creates possible scenarios that, often unique and risky, must be morally justifiable and practicably viable. Moral imagination is thus distinguished from fantasy and from mere creative imaginability, just as Paul Mozer's schemes are distinguished from those of Johnson & Johnson (J&J).

The South Shore Bank development illustrates the integration of moral imagination and moral reasoning. It was enormously imaginative to think that one could create a viable financial institution out of the old South Shore Bank in what appeared to be a hopelessly depressed and increasingly dangerous neighborhood. It took courage and imagination, moral imagination, to engage in a project that no other Chicago bank at that time would consider, in a neighborhood that leading sociologists had written off, particularly when the project is neither government-funded nor a charity but is a for-profit, and profitable, enterprise. The bank began with difficult social conditions and banking regulations. It then reconfigured the framework of traditional "banking logic" to test the hypothesis that they could practice banking in a socially responsible and profitable manner under challenging circumstances. While questioning of traditional sociological and financial wisdom, South Shore Bank's lending practices exhibited practical common sense. The bank reconstituted the criteria for defining fiscally sound loan candidates, but it did not lend money to deadbeats or people who had a questionable work record. Moreover, it charges a fairly high interest rate on all its loans. While taking on what appeared to be an impossible socially responsible mission, South Shore Bank grounded that mission in the practical realization that it could survive and "do good" only if it was profitable. Investors would not continue to pour money into a losing venture, even to save a neighborhood, and part of saving the South Shore neighborhood was saving the bank. Survival, profitability, social responsibility, and neighborhood revival were all intricately related so that the imaginative project could be financially solid and worthwhile.

This case illustrates how imagination provides the means to challenge one's perspective through "pushes" to impartiality that jar one from a particular point of view. *Moral* imagination involves developing less partial and self-critical perspectives. But this is obviously a dynamic, two-way relationship, for being self-critical and at the same time cognizant of one's schema requires lots of imagination on one particular situation. On the other hand, this process is not *just* imaginative. To be morally imaginative, one needs to appeal to good reasons as the basis for evaluation and moral judgments, good reasons supplied by the ideal of an impartial spectator, social moral rules, expectations of common morality, and moral standards.

A fruitful way to think of this approach is to mentally construct a dialogue between sociologists, business people, bank managers, the prevailing investment philosophy of 1973, and South Shore Bank's potential investors. Before buying the South Shore Bank, Ron Grzywinski had been a student at the Stevenson Institute at the University of Chicago and had written a paper showing how a viable neighborhood financial institution is essential to saving a community. His paper intensified the discourses between his thinking and those of his professors and potential investors in his project. This was an imaginative analysis, but with enough solid data to be fiscally viable as well. Grzywinski questioned other theories and challenged those perspectives with others. But this process was not merely artificial because it entailed the practical challenge of revitalizing a financial institution as well as a community. After the Stevenson Institute, Grzywinski went to work as a professional banker at the Hyde Park Bank of Chicago, which, although located on the South Side of Chicago, engaged in traditional lending practices. But Grzywinski did not identify himself with his roles and role obligations, and he saw that Hyde Park's traditional lending policies were insufficient to enhance the neighborhood. Grzywinski combined good reasoning skills with an active imagination; he disengaged himself from traditional banking practices but not from good common sense. Thus, he envisioned and created a profitable, socially responsible development bank.

MORAL REASONING AND MORAL IMAGINATION

Herein lies a temptation—to allow an appeal to a disinterested or impartial spectator to do all the moral work. It is tempting to link impartiality to rationality, and then to argue that an impartial, rational perspective in the moral reasoning process is necessary *and* sufficient for moral decision-making. (See, for example, Gert, 1987.) But an impartial, rational perspective is still a *perspective* from someplace within some conceptual scheme. Nestlé thought it was taking an impartial, rational perspective when it marketed infant formula in East Africa, and from one positionally objective point of view, this was true. And DCC took a scientific positionally objective perceptive when it failed to take into account emotional reports from ill women with implants. In both cases, the company in question failed to imagine another point of view, another way of looking at the set of events which, it turned out, affected the outcome of the issues in question.

There is a second reason why an impartial, rational perspective is not sufficient for moral decision-making. In chapter 2 I argued that moral theory tends to start with the general—general moral principles—and then applies those principles or modes of reasoning to particular cases. The result is often a disconnect between theory and practice, a failure of application due to a failure to comprehend how moral theory relates to the relevant practice.

Analogously, an impartial, rational perspective by itself may separate the moral from the practically realizable, or the ethical from the economic. I have criticized Nestlé for focusing on its product and a previously successful marketing strategy and not on the cultural and economic context of mothers in East Africa. But one could commit the opposite error as well. For example, we could admire South Shore Bank as an exemplary model of a development bank. Yet South Shore Bank, for all its good works, could not have achieved its goals without being fiscally viable, to be fiscally sound it had to develop the neighborhood, in improving the neighborhood it helped many people, in helping people it increased its deposits, and in increasing its deposits it became a profitable development bank.

In studying the Merck case, there is a temptation to focus on Merck's supererogatory act of giving away Mectizan. Yet that act was a result of a reasoning process that took into account Merck's core values, the motivations of its researchers, and previous successes with new discoveries such as antibiotics that Merck gave away to the Japanese after World War II. Because of those gifts, Merck is now the largest drug exporter to Japan. Merck appears to have two traditions: research and development of drugs to cure disease and profitability, both of which are values the company espouses. In thinking about river blindness drug research, Merck officials may have prioritized those values in a way that questioned profitability as its first priority, at least in the very long short term. But while it *appears* that Merck's priority in this case was the moral standard of curing disease when it was within its intellectual and financial capabilities to do so, this standard had always paid off in the past. Even in the river blindness case, as with South Shore Bank, one cannot clearly separate out doing good and doing well. Had Merck decided not to develop Mectizan, this surely would have demoralized its best researchers, whose contributions had made Merck an uncontested leader in the pharmaceutical industry.

New research has recently found that

> [i]n recent clinical trials, a form of Mectizan has been shown to be effective in treating scabies, a skin disease often occurring in people who have been infected with the HIV virus. One oral dose seems to be effective in ridding otherwise healthy patients with scabies, and two or three doses has been effective for those with the HIV virus. (Meinking et al., 1995, 26–30)

In another context, we might find Merck *appearing* to prioritize profitability in choosing investing in the development of certain new drugs. Merck is one of three manufacturers of protease inhibitors for the treatment of HIV-infected patients. Used with the combination of two other drugs, Merck's drug, Crixivan, is highly successful in arresting the HIV virus. A very expensive drug, its yearly treatment cost can reach $20,000 a year. Yet Merck has created a policy that allows indigent HIV-infected patients to apply for free medication when other sources of funding have been exhausted (Pear, 1997, 1, 6).

Merck has become a role model for other pharmaceutical companies as well. This year, SmithKline Beecham announced that it would give away Albendazole, a drug that stops the growth of parasites that cause elephantiasis. If it is taken with ivermectin (Merck's Mectizan), the disease is curable. About 120 million people have elephantiasis, and about 1 billion are at risk of getting the disease. This program will cost SmithKline Beecham approximately $500 million over the next 20 years (Brown, 1998, A1, A5).

The Merck and South Shore Bank cases illustrate R. Edward Freeman's conclusion that what he calls the Separation Thesis—the idea that economics and ethics are two distinct forms of discourse in describing management and corporate practices—is bankrupt because it forces false dilemmas on business practices—mental models that create the illusion that a business can be either morally good or profitable, or that doing good (however one interprets the term "good") and doing well (e.g., providing a large return for shareholders) are often incompatible (Freeman, 1994, 412–43). The Separation Thesis appears in many guises. In earlier chapters I have argued that it is a conceptual mistake to separate the thin self from the thick self, although each aspect is necessary to explain both the social character and the individuality of the self. I have also argued that role morality is insufficient to account for moral responsibility and accountability. That is, role morality makes sense only in the context of a broader conception of morality and moral responsibility. Throughout the book I have argued that one cannot work on moral theory isolated from particular practices and events. Indeed, I have suggested that one must begin with practice, the particular, the thick of situational events. Yet applied ethics is more than situational ethics, just as morality cannot be equated with role morality. It is mistaken to imagine that managers can think and act successfully as if they were in an arena where ethical considerations do not apply. Such a thesis explains why some managers at Nestlé did not understand why Nestlé was blamed for producing and marketing fine products in East Africa. In addition, it is equally mistaken to morally evaluate business without considering the political/economic/social context in which commercial activities occur, admiring South Shore Bank's community development strategies without taking into account the practicalities of achieving and continuing those strategies.[1]

Moral imagination helps each of us to perceive and frame the normative core embedded in all human enterprises including commerce and economics without dividing it from its subject matter and particularities of its practices. Therefore, an idea of a disengaged, reasonable perspective cannot be separated from the idea of moral imagination. Otherwise, one becomes mired in moral theory or in situational economics. That connection between a disengaged, reasonable perspective and moral imagination entails the following:

(1) an awareness of the particular: the character, context, situation, event and dilemma at issue;

(2) awareness of the script or conceptual scheme functioning in that context;

(3) awareness of possible moral conflicts or dilemmas that might arise in that situation, including dilemmas created at least in part by the dominating script, as well as others created by the situation itself;

(4) envisioning possibilities that other reasonable but disengaged persons could envision too, given that situation and the protagonists' roles in that situation.

In a more productive mode, the imaginative reasonable impartial spectator might begin to ask questions such as

(1) Is this dilemma solvable given the parameters of the context, and extant "scripts"?

(2) What are the possibilities that are not context-dependent?

(3) Might we have to revamp the operative script to take into account new possibilities not within the scope of one's particular situation or within one's role in that situation?

And last, creative moral imagination or normative free reflection includes evaluation and revision:

(1) evaluating both the status quo and newly formulated possibilities;

(2) envisioning how morally to justify actualizing new possibilities, appealing now in both cases to moral rules or general principles of morality;

(3) revising operative scripts or even a conceptual scheme that affects particular interpretations of this situation and other similar particular situations; and sometimes

(4) revising social norms, moral rules, or standards themselves in light of new facts or reinterpretations of past and present events.

Every stage of this process involves imagination, disengagement, and evaluation. This process includes appeals to, or alterations of, standards or moral rules while at the same time grounding the decision in what is morally possible and practically achievable.

MORAL MINIMUMS

But we are still left with a question. Are these processes merely constructivist or relativist? One evaluates an event through moral rules that themselves arise out of, depend on, or are reformulated by a particular community or practice. One reformulates mental models or revises a conceptual scheme; still these are context-dependent. A disengaged or constructed view from somewhere is still that—a view from *somewhere,* that is, at best, created from a background of historical context, tradition, and social narratives that cannot be eliminated.

Appealing again to Michael Walzer's work, I shall now introduce another element that will partly respond to this problem. In his well-known book *Spheres of Justice* (1983), Walzer develops a pluralistic and relativistic theory of the good. Walzer argues that who we are and what we value are defined in terms of social goods. Even though social goods may overlap, each social good has its own definition and "sphere" of application, values, and distributive criteria. Because different societies or different groups within a society could have quite disparate social goods, one can define "basic goods, or the human good" only contextually (Walzer, 1983, chapter 1).

In a later book, *Thick and Thin,* Walzer qualifies the relativistic notion of spheres of social goods. He argues that running through the thickness of each sphere of social goods—and, on a larger scale, running through each culture—is a "thin theory of the good," or what Walzer also calls "moral minimums." Walzer is arguing that throughout history and in different cultures spins a thin thread of coherence and agreement. The agreement is less about what is *good,* but rather on at least a partial universal recognition of "bads." For example, Walzer argues, although there is wide disagreement about definitions or theories of justice, there is mutual recognition of *injustice.* We are uncertain about the constitution of the "good life," but there is widespread agreement about deficient or despicable living conditions, indecencies, violations of human rights, mistreatment, and other harms. We all agree that Bhopal and *Challenger* were disasters. We are less certain about how to prevent such future disasters. We know that children should not sniff glue; Fuller's liability and what it should do in Honduras are not as evident. Walzer does not spell out the content of these minimums. I suggest that moral minimums are best understood as negative standards, universally agreed upon "bottom lines" beyond which it is morally questionable to act. For example, it is almost always wrong to deliberately harm or contribute to harming another person or persons; to deliberately violate their rights to freedom, life, or property; to treat individuals or classes of individuals with disrespect; to compete or cooperate unfairly; not to honor promises or contract; or to be dishonest or deceitful. Whereas these moral minimums do not define goodness, fairness, or benefit, or define the positive content of rights, they set minimum guidelines for behavior that most people everywhere might agree on, and the idea of moral minimums gives a strong counterargument to those who find values merely context-dependent (Walzer, 1994).

In a similar vein and applying Walzer's notion of moral minimums to business, Tom Donaldson has developed "moral minimums for multinationals." Donaldson develops a list of basic rights minimally required in any humane society or on any minimally morally decent context. These rights include rights to freedom of movement, speech, political participation, and association; rights to ownership to freedom from torture; rights to a fair trial, nondiscrimination, physical security, minimal education, and subsistence. Donaldson then argues that multinational corporations have duties to avoid depriving any person of these rights. For some of these rights—those of physical security, freedom of speech, minimal education, political participation, and subsistence—Donaldson contends, multinationals have duties to help protect people from deprivation. Although one may debate Donaldson's particular list of rights and duties, his general argument that there are some recognizable and universally acceptable moral minimums for behavior, the violation of which is an agreed-upon wrong, seems sound (Donaldson, 1989b).

The idea of a set of moral minimums presents another temptation, the temptation to declare moral minimums as absolutes. But, the idea that the content of these moral minimums is subject to historical change is consistent with Walzer's thinking. They are not fixed absolutes; rather, they are revisable negative ideals. A moral minimum is a candidate for a universal principle, but never elected for eternity or even for life. In chapter 5 I gave the example of how we have revised moral minimums to include environmental standards as a new moral minimum. Moral minimums explain how we appeal to general principles—but from a context, from a tradition, or as a challenge to a tradition, and never from "nowhere,"—and thus how we revise or change the standards.

The thread of moral minimums is an appeal to standards that are not *merely* products of a particular tradition or a specific historical moment. They provide a limited objectivity so that the process of decision-making and moral judgment is just that, a process, but not a circular one (Brink, 1989, 139–43). The appeal to moral minimums, to these common "threads" of principles that reappear in different historical periods and in disparate cultures is an appeal to impartial standards, albeit impartial within limits of human understanding and imagination. Moreover, moral minimums provide standards with which to judge not merely Joseph Jett, the production of the Pinto and Bronco II, Merck's production of Mectizan, or other similar actions but also one's background narrative and tradition, common sense morality, one's allegedly impartial perspective, and even the minimums themselves.

MORAL IMAGINATION, MORAL REASONING, AND MORAL MINIMUMS

The idea of moral imagination, the background of tradition and custom in which a narrative or situation is embedded, a disengaged view from somewhere, and a thin theory of moral minimums are all central elements of a viable moral decision-making process when that process begins with the specific and particular. One begins with the particular, a particular event or series of events embedded in a culturally, socially, and sometimes institutionally defined context within traditions, laws, customs, narratives, language, and practices that define and help to determine the event. Recognizing that an event poses moral problems is also in part determined by the practice in which the event occurs. So, for example, given its corporate structure and culture, the quality of its products, and its successes in other parts of the world, the Nestlé Corporation did not even recognize a problem in marketing infant formula in developing African countries. Similarly, from a positionally objective point of view, Ford managers did not perceive an issue with Pinto explosions. So recognition of a moral problem involves imaginative disengagement from the situation. Interestingly, even from this disengaged point of view, initial resolutions to the dilemmas discovered in an event are often from a positionally objective point of view as well. H. B. Fuller recognizes that its glue is misused in Honduras and that in Central America its brand name has become the generic name for children who sniff any kind of glue. But the company has not gone beyond that recognition to devise creative, workable solutions to this problem.

Part of the process of taking a disengaged view is to test and evaluate the dilemma and possible solutions. This process entails testing moral judgments in particular contexts against moral minimums in the context of traditions, practices, narratives, conceptual schemes, and other presuppositions out of which decision-making takes place. One begins with a decision, to manufacture glue in Honduras. One tests alternatives first against the background tradition and practice of the situation (e.g., the Honduras culture, economy, and workforce; US customs, mores, common sense morality, and laws). Taking a more impartial perspective, one tests alternatives against the wider background of culture, tradition, and relationships of those affected by the production glue, for example, employees, suppliers, wholesalers, and end users of the product. Third, one tests the decision possibilities against negative moral minimums. Who is harmed? What if the glue is misused? What sorts of measures does Honduras have to prevent misuse? Does Fuller need to manufacture glue in Central America? Does the loss of jobs created by closing the glue factory create more harm than its misuse on the street? In these processes moral imagination, the ability to conceive of, envision, evaluate, and actualize new possibilities, plays a key role.

Sometimes demands of a particular set of events require more imagination and judgment. In the *Challenger* disaster, everyone acted with the best intentions, yet there was an explosion. That case required reformulation of the mental models operative at Thiokol and at NASA to enable

an understanding of disparate points of view. At Salomon Brothers, I
suggest that it took the Paul Mozer scandal and the intervention of its
primary stockholder, Warren Buffett, to change the mental model operating on its trading floor. In reformulating one's mental models, one
again has to evaluate alternatives that follow from rethinking a problem
through a new framework. This is exemplified by the actions of Robert
Haas at Levi Strauss when he rethought that company's China policy by
developing a fresh way to analyze that opportunity.

This set of solutions to a particular dilemma becomes an example, a
model for further similar moral judgments. Given the Nestlé problem,
other companies should use that example as a warning when they introduce products into developing countries. Given the *Challenger* tragedy,
NASA and Thiokol have altered their thinking about the safety of space
travel. After the Lockheed/Japan incident, Lockheed, now Lockheed-
Martin, developed an ethics program and revamped its corporate decision processes, today priding itself as being in the forefront of creative
moral decision-making in the aerospace industry.

Finally, given a particular set of recurring events and a very active disengaged imagination, one begins to examine and sometimes revise the
moral rules or precepts of common morality themselves. In an earlier
chapter I offered the example of how we have revised our moral standards concerning responsibility to the environment. Let me give an example from politics. It took many centuries of political dialogue to arrive at what developed into the American Constitution. One of the
rights proposed by the Constitution is the right of every adult to vote.
Originally interpreted, this was interpreted as the right of every adult
white, non-Catholic, property-owning male to vote. Gradually, however,
practices changed, and today, with the help of the 15th, 19th, and 26th
amendments, this right is guaranteed to all adult citizens of all races,
genders, ethnic origins, and religious commitments who are 18 or
older. This interpretation of the right to vote has reached an equilibrium; that is, we no longer challenge it, and almost no one conceives of
reverting to property rights or gender as defining a right to vote. What
we have done, over time, is to redefine the content of the right to vote to
make it more inclusive, and this right, as presently interpreted, has become a model to which other nations appeal in setting their own standards. This does not mean that sometime in the future we will not again
revisit this right and reinterpret it further; indeed, we are in the process
of extending that right to the homeless. This is a tentative universal standard, a candidate, but, momentarily at least, this right is no longer
morally challenged.

In the case of constitutional rights to vote, we have reached a stage of
equilibrium, no longer challenging this right. According to *Webster's Col-
legiate Dictionary* equilibrium is "a state of balance, poise, a state of ad-

justment between opposing or divergent influences or elements, a state of balance between opposing forces or actions that is either static or dynamic." Occasionally, one does reach a state of moral equilibrium wherein succeeding events do not present a challenge but rather are solvable because of past moral judgments. It is a process, the aim of which is not unlike what John Rawls and Norman Daniels call wide reflective equilibrium. Rawls summarizes this process:

> [B]y going back and forth [between the particular and principles], sometimes altering the conditions of the contractual circumstances, at others withdrawing our judgments and conforming them to principle, I assume that eventually we shall find a description of the initial situation [solution or set of solutions to the decision process] that both expresses reasonable conditions and yields principles which match our considered judgments duly pruned and adjusted. (Rawls, 1971, 48; see also Daniels, 1979)

The process of moral decision-making I have just described that takes into account context and tradition, impartiality, and minimum moral standards, is just that: a process, a dynamic process, in which one challenges the presuppositions of tradition, tests one's impartiality against context, and continues to shape one's decisions and refine one's moral minimums. Moral judgments are a result of a delicate balance of context, evaluation, the projection of moral minimums, and the presence or absence of imagination. Such a process is seldom complete, pure objectivity is impossible, but infallibility of judgment is not part of the goal. Indeed, moral judgments are at best partial solutions. Still, they should be solutions that serve as the starting place or models for new series of decisions, as the latest SmithKline Beecham decision illustrates, even though these, too, are always at risk of being morally challenged. The linchpin of this process is a highly developed moral imagination that perceives the nuances of a situation, challenges the framework or scheme in which the event is embedded, and imagines how that situation and other similar situations might be different. The ideal is not absolute agreement but rather temporary equilibrium, a dynamic consensus that provides the ground and impetus for moral progress.

The working of moral imagination can be summarized concisely in a statement that is reportedly the favorite religious expression of Aaron Feuerstein (Goozner, 1996, 27): "Who is honored? One who honors others."

NOTES

1. Introduction

1. GE subsequently divested itself of Kidder.

2. Moral amnesia is not limited to business. Recently the World Medical Association elected Dr. Hans Hoachim Sewering, an active participant in the Nazi medical profession's euthanasia activities during World War II, to its presidency. It apparently forgot about Dr. Sewering's past medical interests. When this became public knowledge, the election was annulled (Leaning, 1993, A11).

2. Some Partial Solutions

1. While Kohlberg chooses secular principles—utility, rights, and justice—the world's great religions set out general moral principles as well. (Indeed, religion probably started this trend.)

2. This idea was pointed out to me by John Dienhart.

3. This sort of behavior does not happen only in business. One will recall a particularly dreadful incident during the Vietnam War. On March 6, 1968, Captain Ernest L. Medina and Lt. William L. Calley, both United States Marine officers, led a battalion of Marines into the village of My Lai, and, according to reports, instructed their men to kill the civilians in that village, including women and children, despite the questionable proof of their involvement with the Viet Cong. When questioned afterward during his court martial proceedings (he was first found guilty, later pardoned), Calley argued that he was just following the orders of his commanding officers and doing his duty during a wartime situation (Bilton and Sim, 1992).

Adolph Eichmann is a more infamous character. Eichmann was a clerk in Nazi Germany during World War II. His primary responsibility was the railroad transportation of Jews and other condemned persons to concentration camps. Eichmann was a meticulous employee. His trains ran on time, the cars were always full—no empty spaces—and he kept detailed records of the names and ethnic origins of those going to the camps.

Some 15 years after the war, Eichmann was captured by the Israelis and brought to trial in Israel for war crimes. At the trial he pleaded innocent, arguing that he was doing his duty, obeying orders and the law, particularly the law of the German state. He even declared that he was acting from a sense of Kantian moral imperative, always doing his duty with respect to what he believed to be general (even universal) law. His only pangs of conscience were because he actually helped some half-Jewish relatives escape, thus disobeying what he took to be his exceptionless duties to the Third Reich. Eichmann was also proud of the fact that during the last days of the war when the Nazis, realizing their imminent defeat, tried to cover up the Final Solution activities, he objected and continued sending victims to death camps in Hungary as long as he could (Arendt, 1963, 135–40).

3. "The Very Idea of a Conceptual Scheme"

The title is taken from Donald Davidson's well-known essay "On the Very Idea of a Conceptual Scheme," *Proceedings of the American Philosophical Association*, 48 (1974), 5–20.

1. I use the term "was" because in 1989 Morton divested itself of the rocket booster division of Thiokol, and Thiokol is now an independent company.

2. However, neither Putnam nor Rorty would defend the incommensurability argument.

3. Davidson would disagree with this conclusion, because he tries to argue that there really are not great differences between conceptual schemes. I find the idea of a conceptual scheme to be an enormously valuable idea to explain how we each perceive and shape the world in sometimes fundamentally different ways while at the same time we are capable of understanding these very fundamental differences.

4. The *Rashomon* Effect

1. According to Marcia Angell, approximately 80% of all breast implant surgeries are done for cosmetic reasons. About 20% are reconstructions after mastectomies (Angell, 1996, 19).

6. Moral Reasoning and Moral Imagination

1. John Dienhart nicely summarized this point for me.

BIBLIOGRAPHY

Alexander, Garth. 1994. "The Man Who Kidded Kidder for $350 Million." *New York Times*. April 24, B1.

Andre, Judith. 1991. "Role Morality as a Complex Instance of Ordinary Morality." *American Philosophical Quarterly*. 28: 73–80.

Angell, Marcia. 1995. "Are Breast Implants Actually OK?" *New Republic*. September 11, 17–21.

————. 1996 *Science on Trial*. New York: W. W. Norton.

Anscombe. G. E. M. 1976. "The Question of Linguistic Idealism." In Jaakko Hintikka, ed., *Essays on Wittgenstein in Honour of G. H. Von Wright*. Acta Philosophica Fennica, vol. 28. Amsterdam: North Holland Publishing. 181–215.

Arendt, Hannah. 1963. *Eichmann in Jerusalem*. New York: Viking Press.

Bacon, Kenneth H., and Kevin G. Salwen. 1991. "Summer of Financial Scandals Raises Questions about the Ability of Regulators to Police Markets." *Wall Street Journal*. August 28, A10.

Bartlett, Sarah. 1991. "Salomon's Errant Cowboy." *New York Times*. August 25, C1.

Bebeau, Muriel J. 1994. "Influencing the Moral Dimensions of Dental Practice." In James Rest et al., eds. *Moral Development in the Professions*. Hillsdale, NJ: Lawrence Erlbaum. 121–146.

Beidelman, T. O. 1986. *Moral Imagination in Kaguru Modes of Thought*. Bloomington: Indiana University Press.

Bell, T. E., and K. Ech. 1989. "The Fatal Flaw in Flight 51-L." *IEEE Spectrum*. 24: 36–51.

Bentham, Jeremy. 1789; 1948. *An Introduction to the Principles of Morals and Legislation*. New York: Hafner.

Bilton, Michael, and Kevin Sim. 1992. *Four Hours in My Lai*. New York: Viking Press.

Boesky, Ivan. 1986. Commencement Address to the Haas School of Management, University of California at Berkeley. May 18.

Boisjoly, Roger. 1988. "Interview: Whistleblower." *Life.* 11(13): 17–22.

Boisjoly, Russell, Ellen Foster Curtis, and Eugene Mellicana. 1989. "Roger Boisjoly and the Challenger Disaster: The Ethical Dimensions." *Journal of Business Ethics.* 8: 217–230.

Bollier, David. 1996. *Aiming Higher.* New York: American Management Association.

Bollier, David, Stephanie Weiss, and Kirk O. Hanson. "Merck and Co." Harvard University Graduate School of Business Administration Case #9-991-021. Boston: Harvard Business School Press.

Bowie, Norman, and Stephanie Lenway. "H. B. Fuller in Honduras: Street Children and Substance Abuse." In Thomas Donaldson and Patricia H. Werhane, eds. *Ethical Issues in Business.* Fourth Edition. Englewood Cliffs, NJ: Prentice Hall, 1993. 24–38.

Brann, Eva T. H. 1991. *The World of the Imagination: Sum and Substance.* Totowa, NJ: Rowman and Littlefield.

Brink, David. 1989. *Moral Realism and the Foundations of Ethics.* Cambridge: Cambridge University Press.

Brown, David. 1998. "Company to Donate Drug to Fight Tropical Parasite." *Washington Post.* February 3, A1, A5.

Brinton, Louise A., and S. Lori Brown. 1997. "Breast Implants and Cancer." *Journal of the National Cancer Institute.* 89: 1341–1349.

Burrough, Paul. 1990. *Barbarians at the Gate.* New York: Harper & Row.

Burton, Thomas M. 1996. "Breast Implant Study is Fresh Fuel for Debate." *Wall Street Journal.* February 28, B1, B4.

Byrne, John A. 1995. "Informed Consent." *Business Week.* October 2, 104–116.

———. 1996 Informed Consent: A Story of Personal Tragedy and Corporate Betrayal. New York: McGraw-Hill.

Callahan, Joan, ed. 1988. *Ethical Issues in Professional Life.* New York: Oxford University Press.

Carey, John. 1996. "Breast-Implant Cases: Let the Science Testify." *Business Week.* December 16, 2.

Carroll, Archie. 1987. "In Search of the Moral Manager. *Business Horizons.* 30: 7–25.

Castleman, Michael. 1998. "Implanted Evidence." *Mother Jones.* Jan/Feb, 25–26.

Chambers, Tod. 1996. "From an Ethicist's Point of View: The Literary Nature of Ethical Inquiry." *Hastings Center Report.* 26: 25–33.

Chomsky, Noam. 1965. *Aspects of the Theory of Syntax.* Cambridge, MA: MIT Press.

Churchland, Paul. 1989. *A Neurocomputational Perspective.* Cambridge, MA: MIT Press.

Ciulla, Joanne. 1998. "Imagination, Fantasy, Wishful Thinking and Truth." *Business Ethics Quarterly,* forthcoming.

Cohen, Laurie P., Alix M. Freedman, and William Power. 1994. "Growing Mess: Kidder's No. 2 Man Comes Under Scrutiny in Trading Scandal." *Wall Street Journal.* May 2, A1, A8.

Coleridge, Samuel Taylor. 1907; 1973. *Biographia Literaria, Volumes I and II.* Ed. J. Shawcross. London: Oxford University Press.

Collins, James C., and Jerry I. Porras. 1994. *Built to Last.* New York: HarperBusiness.

Dancy, R. M. 1983. "Alien Concepts." *Synthese.* 56: 283–300.

Daniels, Norman. 1979. "Wide Reflective Equilibrium and Theory Acceptance in Ethics." *Journal of Philosophy.* 76: 256–281.

Davidson, Dekkers, and Kenneth E. Goodpaster. 1983. "Managing Product Safety: The Ford Pinto." Harvard University Graduate School of Business Administration Case # 9-383-129. Boston: Harvard Business School Press.

Davidson, Donald. 1974. "On the Very Idea of a Conceptual Scheme." *Proceedings and Addresses of the American Philosophical Association.* 47: 5–20.

Davis, Michael. 1987. "Why Engineers Should Support Their Profession's Code." Speech to the Society of Hispanic Professional Engineers. June 10.

———. 1989. "Explaining Wrongdoing." *Journal of Social Philosophy,* 20: 74–90.

Derry, Robbin. 1989. "An Empirical Study of Moral Reasoning Among Managers." *Journal of Business Ethics.* 8: 855–862.

Dewey, John. 1958. *Art as Excperience.* New York: Capricorn.

Diamond, Cora. 1991. "Missing the Adventure." *The Realistic Spirit.* Cambridge, MA: MIT Press. 309–318.

Dirks, Raymond L., and Leonard Gross. 1974. *The Great Wall Street Scandal.* New York: McGraw Hill.

Donaldson, Thomas. 1989a. *The Ethics of International Business.* New York: Oxford University Press.

———. 1989b. "Moral Minimums for Multinationals." *Ethics and International Affairs.* 3: 163–182.

Dowie, Mark. 1977a. "How Ford Put Two Million Firetraps on Wheels." *Business and Society Review.* 23: 46–55.

———. 1977b. "Pinto Madness." *Mother Jones.* September/October, 18–32.

Downie, R. S. 1971. *Roles and Values.* London: Methuen.

Drake, Philip D., and John W. Peavy. 1995. "Fundamental Analysis, Stock Prices, and the Demise of MiniScribe Corporation." *Journal of Portfolio Management,* 21: 68–73.

Driscoll, Dawn-Marie, W. Michael Hoffman, and Edward Petry. 1995. "Dow Corning: First, Kill All the Lawyers." *The Ethical Edge.* New York: MasterMedia Limited. 127–141.

Dyer, Andrew D., Todd E. Himstead, and Craig N. Smith. 1995. "Dow Corning Corporation: Marketing Breast Implant Devices." Washington, DC: Georgetown University School of Business.

Earl, Peter. 1984. *The Corporate Imagination.* Armonk, NY: M.E. Sharpe.

———. 1983. *The Economic Imagination.* Brighton, England: Wheatsheaf.

Emmet, Dorothy. 1966. *Rules, Roles and Relation.* New York: St. Martin's Press.

Ermarth, E. 1991. *Sequel to History.* Princeton: Princeton University Press.

Esty, Benjamin. 1995. "South Shore Bank: Is it The Model of Success for Community Development Banks?" Harvard Business School Working Paper 95-072. Boston: Harvard Business School Press.

Feynman, Richard. 1989. *What Do You Care What Other People Think.* New York: W. W. Norton.

Flax, Robert A., and Patricia H. Werhane. 1997. "Dow Corning and Informed Consent." *Darden Case Bibliography, UVA-E-0105-0106.* Charlottesville, VA: Darden School, University of Virginia.

"Ford Fights Pinto Case: Jury Gives 128 Million." 1978. *Auto News.* February 13.

Frantz, Douglas, and Sylvia Nasar. 1994. "F.B.I. Inquiry on Jet Engine, New Jolt to Company Images." *New York Times.* July 18, A1.

Freeman, R. Edward. 1994. "The Politics of Stakeholder Theory: Some Future Directions." *Business Ethics Quarterly.* 4: 409–422.

Friedman, Marilyn. 1993. *What are Friends For?* Ithaca, NY: Cornell University Press.

Gabriel, S. E. et al. 1994. "Risk of Connective-Tissue Diseases and Other Disorders After Breast Implantation." *New England Journal of Medicine.* 330: 1697–1702.

Galston, William A. 1991. *Liberal Purposes.* Cambridge: Cambridge University Press.

Geertz, Clifford. 1973. *The Interpretation of Cultures.* New York: Basic Books.

———. 1983. *Local Knowledge.* New York: Basic Books.

Gentner, Dedre, and Eric W. Whitley. 1997. "Mental Models of Population Growth." In Max H. Bazerman, David M. Messick, Ann E. Tenbrunsel, and Kimberley A. Wade-Benzoni, eds., *Environment, Ethics, and Behavior.* San Francisco: New Lexington Press.

Gert, Bernard. 1987. *Morality.* New York: Oxford University Press.

Geyelin, Milo, and Neal Templin. 1993. "Legal Maneuvers: Ford Attorneys Played Unusually Large Role in Bronco II's Launch." *Wall Street Journal.* January 5, A1, A6.

Gilligan. Carol. 1982. *In a Different Voice.* Cambridge, MA: Harvard University Press.

———. 1986. "Symbols, Scripts, and Sensemaking." In H. P. Sims, Jr., and Dennis Gioia, eds., *The Thinking Organization.* San Francisco: Jossey-Bass. 49–74.

Gioia, Dennis. 1992. "Pinto Fires and Personal Ethics: A Script Analysis of Missed Opportunities." *Journal of Business Ethics.* 11: 379–389.

Gioia, Dennis, and Evelyn Pitré. 1990. "Multiparadigm Perspectives on Theory Building." *Academy of Management Review.* 15: 584–602.

Gioia, Dennis, and P. P. Poole. 1984. "Scripts in Organizational Behavior." *Academy of Management Review.* 9: 449–459.

Giltay, Erik J. et al. 1994. "Silicone Breast Prostheses and Rheumatic Symptoms: A Retrospective Follow Up Study." *Annals of Rheumatic Diseases.* 53: 194–196.

Goffman, Erving. 1961. *Encounters: Two Studies in the Sociology of Interaction.* Indianapolis: Bobbs-Merrill.

Goldman, Alan. 1980. *The Moral Foundations of Professional Ethics.* Totowa, NJ: Rowman and Littlefield.

Gombrich, E. H. 1961. *Art and Illusion.* Princeton: Princeton University Press.

Goozner, Merrill. 1996. "The *Mensch* of Malden Mills Inspires." *Chicago Tribune.* December 26, 1, 27.

Gorman, Michael. 1992. *Simulating Science.* Bloomington: Indiana University Press.

Grimshaw v. Ford Motor Co. 1978. No. 197761. Super CT. Orange County, CA, February 6.

Gryzwinski, Ronald. 1991. "The New Old-Fashioned Banking." *Harvard Business Review.* 69: 87–98.

Guroian, Vigen. 1996. "Awakening the Moral Imagination." *Intercollegiae Review.* 32: 3–13.

Halliday, Bronwyn, and Lynn Sharp Paine. 1992. "Beech-Nut Nutrition Corporation." Harvard Graduate School of Business Administration Case #9-392-084. Boston: Harvard Business School Press.

Hansell, Saul. 1994. "Kidder Reports Fraud and Ousts a Top Trader." *New York Times.* April 18, A1.

Hardimon, Michael. 1994. "Role Obligations." *Journal of Philosophy.* 91: 333–363.

Harre, Rom, ed. 1986. *The Social Construction of Emotions.* Oxford: Oxford University Press.

Heisenberg, Werner. 1959. *Physics and Philosophy.* London: George Allen & Unwin, Ltd.

Hill, G. Christian. 1990. "A Never Ending Story." *Stanford Law and Policy.* 2: 21–36.

Himmelfarb, Gertrude. 1991. *Poverty and Compassion: The Moral Imagination of the Late Victorians.* New York: Knopf.

Hoffman, Michael. 1984. "The Ford Pinto." Rpt. in Lisa H. Newton and Maureen M. Ford, eds., *Taking Sides.* Guilford, CT: Dushkin Publishing Group. 132–137.

Holloway, Nigel. 1995. "Melting Pot." *Far Eastern Economic Review.* May 18: 95–96.

Holusha, John. 1996. "Pulp Mills Turn Over a New Leaf." *New York Times.* March 9, A35–37.

Irwin, Eleanor. 1974. *Colour Terms in Early Greek Poetry.* Toronto: A. M. Hakkert.

Jackson, Norman, and Pippa Carter. 1991. "In Defense of Paradigm Incommensurability." *Organization Studies.* 12: 109–127.

James, Henry. 1934. *The Art of the Novel.* New York: Scribner's.

Janis, I. L. 1982. *Groupthink.* Boston: Houghton and Mifflin.

Johnson, Mark. 1985. "Imagination in Moral Judgment." *Philosophy and Phenomenological Research.* 46: 265–280.

———. 1993. *Moral Imagination.* Chicago: University of Chicago Press.

Kamm, Judith. 1993. "Ethics Officers Gaining Acceptance at Many Firms, Survey Reveals." *Ethikos.* January/February, 7–12.

Kant, Immanuel. 1781; 1970. *Critique of Pure Reason.* Trans. Norman Kemp Smith. London: Macmillan.

———. 1790; 1951. *Critique of Judgment.* Trans. J. H. Bernard. New York: Hafner.

———. 1784; 1959. *The Foundations of the Metaphysics of Morals.* Trans. Lewis White Beck. Indianapolis: Bobbs-Merrill.

———. 1789; 1985. *The Critique of Practical Reason.* Trans. Lewis White Beck. New York: Macmillan.

Katz, Jane Palley, and Lynn Sharp Paine. 1994. "Levi Strauss & Co.: Global Sourcing." Harvard University Graduate School of Business Administration Case # 9-395-f. Boston: Harvard Business School Press. 127, 128.

Kekes, John. 1991. "Moral Imagination, Freedom, and the Humanities." *American Philosophical Quarterly.* 28: 101–111.

———. 1993. *The Morality of Pluralism.* Princeton: Princeton University Press.

Kelly, G. A. 1955. *The Psychology of Personal Constructs.* New York: Norton.

Kessler, David. 1992. "The Basis for the FDA's Decision on Breast Implants." *New England Journal of Medicine.* 326: 1713–1715.

Kohlberg, Lawrence. 1969. "Stage and Sequence: The Cognitive-Development Approach to Socialization." In D. A. Goslin, ed., *Handbook of Socialization Theory and Research.* Chicago: Rand-McNally. 347–380.

————. 1981. *The Philosophy of Moral Development: Moral Stages and the Idea of Justice*. San Francisco: Harper & Row.

Kohlberg, Lawrence, Charles Levine, and Alexandra Hewer. 1983. *Moral Stages: A Current Formulation and a Response to Critics*. New York: Karger.

Kolata, Gina. 1995a. "A Case of Justice or a Total Travesty? *New York Times*. May 28, C1, C6.

————. 1995b. "Proof of a Breast Implant Peril is Lacking, Rheumatologists Say." *New York Times*. October 25: A11.

————. 1995c. "Will the Lawyers Kill Off Norplant?" *New York Times*. May 28: A1.

Kolata, Gina, and Barry Meier. 1995. "Implant Lawsuits Create a Medical Rush to Cash In." *New York Times*. September 18: A1.

Kossovsky, Nir. 1993. "Surface Dependent Antigens Identified by High Binding Avidity of Serum Antibodies in a Subpopulation of Patients with Breast Implants." *Journal of Applied Biomaterials*. 4: 281–288.

————. 1994. "Immunology of Silicone Breast Implants." *Journal of Biomaterials Applications*. 8: 237–246.

Kotchian, Carl. 1977. "The Payoff: Lockheed's 70-Day Million to Tokyo." *Saturday Review*. July 9, 7–12.

Kuhn, Thomas. 1962; 1970. *The Structure of Scientific Revolutions*. Chicago: University of Chicago Press.

Langer, Suzanne. 1942; 1951. *Philosophy in a New Key*. Harvard: Harvard University Press.

Lappé, Marc. 1993. "Silicone-Reactive Disorder: A New Autoimmune Disease Caused by Immunostimulation and Superantigens." *Medical Hypotheses*. 41: 348–352.

Larmore, Charles. 1981. "Moral Judgment." *Review of Metaphysics*. 35: 275–296.

Leaning, Jennifer. 1993. "German Doctors and Their Secrets." *New York Times*. February 6, 11.

Levinas, Immanuel. 1979. *Totality and Infinity*. Trans. Alphonso Lingis. The Hague: Nijoff.

Lewis, Michael. 1989. *Liar's Poker*. New York: W. W. Norton.

Lovibond, Sabina. 1983. *Realism and Imagination in Ethics*. Oxford: Basil Blackwell.

Luben, David. 1988. *Lawyers and Justice*. Princeton: Princeton University Press.

MacIntyre, Alasdair. 1981. After Virtue. Notre Dame, IN: Notre Dame University Press.

Mack, Gracian. 1994. "Joseph Jett Sparks Media Frenzy." Black Enterprise. August 28.

Maier, Mark. 1994. "Challenger: The Path to Disaster." Case Research Journal. 4: 1–155.

————. 1992. "A Major Malfunction." *The Story Behind the Space Shuttle Challenger Disaster*. Videotape Part 2. SEHD. Binghamton, NY: SUNY.

Makkreel, Rudolf. 1990. *Imagination and Interpretation in Kant*. Chicago: University of Chicago Press.

May, Larry. 1996. *The Responsive Self*. Chicago: University of Chicago Press.

McCarthy, Michael J., and Douglas Lavin. 1993. "GM Ordered by Jury to Pay $105.2 Million Over Death." *Wall Street Journal*. February 5, A2.

McCollough, Thomas. 1991. *The Moral Imagination and the Public Life*. Chatham, NJ: Chatham House.

McLaughlin, Joseph K., and Joseph F. Fraumeni, Jr. 1994. "Correspondence Re: Breast Implants, Cancer, and Systemic Sclerosis." *Journal of the National Cancer Institute*. 86: 1424.

McMillan, Sheila, Elizabeth Powell, and Patricia Werhane. 1998. "South Shore Bank." University of Virginia Darden Graduate School of Business Administration Case #E-0148. Charlottesville, VA: Darden School, University of Virginia.

Mehalik, Matthew M., Michael E. Gorman, Andrea Larson, and Patricia H. Werhane. "Design Tex, Incorporated." University of Virginia Darden Graduate School of Business Administration Case #E-0099. Charlottesville, VA: Darden School, University of Virginia.

Meinking, T. L., D. Taplin, J. L. Hermida, R. Pardo, and F. A. Kerdel. 1995. "The Treatment of Scabies with Invermectin." *New England Journal of Medicine*. 333: 26–30.

Messick, David, and Max Bazerman. 1996. "Ethical Leadership and the Psychology of Decision Making." *Sloan Management Review*. 37: 9–23.

Milgram, Stanley. 1969. *Obedience to Authority*. New York: Harper & Row.

Mitchell, Russell, and Michael O'Neal. 1994. "Managing by Values." *Business Week*. August 1, 46–52.

Murray, Alan. 1991. "The Outlook: Salomon Scandal Calls for Auction Overhaul." *Wall Street Journal*. August 26, A1.

Nagel, Thomas. 1986. *The View From Nowhere*. New York: Oxford University Press.

Narva, Richard. 1996. "The Real Story on Malden Mills." *NetMarquee*, httpc.// nmq.com.

Neal, James. 1980. "Closing Argument." *State of Indiana v. Ford Motor Company*, no. 11-431, Cir. Ct., Pulaski, IN.

Norton, David L. 1996. *Imagination, Understanding, and the Virtue of Liberality*. Totowa, NJ: Rowman and Littlefield.

Novitz, David. 1987. *Knowledge, Fiction, and Imagination*. Philadelphia: Temple University Press.

Nussbaum, Martha. 1986. *The Fragility of Goodness*. Cambridge: Cambridge University Press.

———. 1990. *Love's Knowledge*. New York: Oxford University Press.

Paré, Terence P. 1994. "Jack Welch's Nightmare on Wall Street," *Fortune*. September 5, 40–47.

Pear, Robert. 1997. "Expense Means Many Can't Get Drugs for AIDS." *New York Times*. February 16, 1, 36.

Peters, Thomas J., and Robert H. Waterman, Jr. 1982. *In Search for Excellence*. New York: Harper & Row.

Powers, Charles, and David Vogel. 1980. *Ethics in the Education of Business Managers*. Hastings-on-Hudson, NY: The Hastings Center.

Price, Martin. 1983. *Forms of Life: Character and Moral Imagination in the Novel*. New Haven: Yale University Press.

Putnam, Hilary. 1990. *Realism With a Human Face*. Cambridge, MA: Harvard University Press.

Railton, Peter. 1986. "Moral Realism." *Philosophical Review*. 95: 168–175.

Rawls, John. 1971. *A Theory of Justice*. Cambridge, MA: Harvard University Press.

Remey, Christine C., and J. Gregory Dees. 1993. "Shorebank Corporation." Harvard University Graduate School of Business Administration Case #9-393-096. Boston: Harvard Business School Press.

Report of the Presidential Commission on the Space Shuttle Challenger Accident, Volumes 1 and 2. 1986.

Rest, James R. 1988. "Can Ethics Be Taught to Adults?" In Lisa H. Newton and Maureen M. Ford, eds., *Taking Sides.* Gilford, CT: Dushkin Publishing Group. 22–26.

———. 1994. "Background: Theory and Research." *Moral Development in the Professions.* Hillside, NJ: Lawrence Erlbaum. 1–26.

Rest, James R., and Darcia Naváez, eds. 1994. *Moral Development in the Professions.* Hillside, NJ: Lawrence Erlbaum.

Ricoeur, Paul. 1979. "The Metaphysical Process as Cognition, Imagination and Feeling." In Sheldon Sacks, ed., *On Metaphor.* Chicago: University of Chicago Press. 141–157.

Rorty, Amelie. 1980. *Explaining Emotions.* Berkeley: University of California Press.

Rorty, Richard. 1993. "Putnam and the Relativist Menace." *Journal of Philosophy.* 90: 443–561.

Rossi, Philip J. 1980. "Moral Interest and Moral Imagination in Kant." *Modern Schoolman.* 58: 149–158.

Rouse, William B., and Nancy M. Morris. 1986. "On Looking Into the Black Box: Prospects and Limits in the Search for Mental Models." *Psychological Bulletin.* 100: 349–363.

Sandel, Michael. 1983. *Liberalism and the Limits of Justice.* Cambridge: Cambridge University Press.

Sanchez-Guerrero, Jorge et al. 1995. "Silicone Breast Implants and the Risk of Connective-Tissue Diseases and Symptoms." *New England Journal of Medicine.* 332: 1666–1670.

Sartre, Jean-Paul. 1956. *Being and Nothingness.* Trans Hazel Barnes. New York: Philosophical Library.

Schmitt, Michael A., and William W. May. 1979. "Beyond Products Liability: The Legal, Social, and Ethical Problems Facing the Automobile Industry in Producing Safe Products." *University of Detroit Journal of Urban Law.* 56: 1021–1050.

Schwartz, Howard. 1987. "On the Psychodynamics of Organizational Disaster." *Columbia Journal of World Business.* 2: 56–67.

———. 1988. "The Symbol of the Space Shuttle and the Degeneration of the American Dream." *Journal of Organizational Change Management.* 1: 5–20.

———. 1990. *Narcissistic Process and Corporate Decay.* New York: New York University Press.

Sen, Amartya. 1993. "Positional Objectivity." *Philosophy and Public Affairs.* 22: 119–130.

Senge, Peter. 1990. *The Fifth Discipline.* New York: Doubleday.

Sethi, S. Prakash. 1994. *Multinational Corporations and the Impact of Public Advocacy on Corporate Strategy.* Dordrecht: Kluwer Academic Publishers.

Shackle, G. L. S. 1979. *Imagination and the Nature of Choice.* Edinburgh: Edinburgh University Press.

Shrivastava, Paul. 1987. *Bhopal: Anatomy of a Crisis.* Cambridge: Ballinger Publishing Company.

Siconolfi, Michael. 1994. "Bond Epic: How Kidder, a Tiger in April, Found Itself the Prey by December." *Wall Street Journal.* December 29, A1, A4.

Smith, Adam. 1759, 1791; 1976. *The Theory of Moral Sentiments.* Ed. A. L. Macfie and D. D. Raphael. Oxford: Oxford University Press.

————. 1763, 1776; 1978. *Lectures on Jurisprudence (A) and (B).* Ed. R. L. Meek, D. D. Raphael, and P. G. Stein. Oxford: Oxford University Press.

————. 1776, 1791; 1976. *The Wealth of Nations.* Ed. R. H. Campbell and A. S. Skinner. Oxford: Oxford University Press.

Smith, Wendy K., and Richard S. Tedlow. 1989. "James Burke: A Career in American Business." Harvard University Graduate School of Business Administration Case #9-389-177. Boston: Harvard Business School Press.

Solomon, Robert. 1992. *Ethics and Excellence.* New York: Oxford University Press.

Starbuck, W. H., and F. J. Milliken. 1988a. "Challenger: Fine-Tuning the Odds Until Something Breaks." *Journal of Management Studies.* 25: 319–340.

————. 1988b. "Executives' Perceptual Filters: What They Notice and How They Make Sense." In Starbuck and Milliken, eds., *The Executive Effect: Concepts and Methods for Studying Top Executives.* Greenwich CT: JAL Press.

State of Indiana v. Ford Motor Co. 1979. No. 11-431. Cir. Ct. Pulaski, IN.

Stein, Barry A., and Rosabeth Moss Kanter. 1993. "Why Good People do Bad Things: A Retrospective on the Hubble Fiasco." *Academy of Management Executive.* 7: 58–62.

Stigler, George. 1971. "Smith's Travels on the Ship of State." *History of Political Economy.* 3: 621–638.

Stocker, Julie, Michael Gorman, and Patricia H. Werhane. 1997. "Dow Corning Corporation Breast Implant Design." *Darden Case Bibliography, UVA-E-0104.* Charlottesville, VA: Darden School, University of Virginia.

Sturdivant, Frederick D., and Larry M. Robinson. 1977. *The Corporate Social Challenge.* Homewood, IL: Irwin.

Swazey, Judith. 1996. "Informed Consent Standards and Practices for Implantable Medical Devices." Bar Harbor, Maine: Acadia Institute.

Taub, Richard. 1988. *Community Capitalism.* Boston: Harvard Business School Press.

Taubes, Gary. 1995. "Silicone in the System." *Discover.* December, 65–75.

Tichy, Noel M., and Stratford Sherman. 1993. Control Your Destiny or Someone Else Will. New York: HarperCollins.

Tierney, Nathan L. 1994. *Imagination and Ethical Ideals.* Albany: State University of New York Press.

Tivnan, Edward. 1995. *The Moral Imagination.* New York: Simon & Schuster.

Trilling, Lionel. 1972. *Sincerity and Authenticity.* Cambridge, MA: Harvard University Press.

————. 1976. *The Liberal Imagination.* New York: Scribner.

Tronto, Joan. 1994. *Moral Boundaries.* New York: Routledge, Chapman, and Hall.

Tuan, Yi-Fu. 1989. *Morality and Imagination.* Madison: University of Wisconsin Press.

U. S. Food and Drug Administration. 1991. "Silicone Gel-Filled Breast Prostheses: Silicone Inflatable Breast Prostheses: Patient Risk Information." *Federal Register,* 56(September 26): 49098–49099.

Vanderford, Marsha L., and David H. Smith. 1997. *The Silicone Breast Implant Story: Communication and Uncertainty.* Hillsdale, NJ: Lawrence Erlbaum.

Vargish, Thomas. 1991. "The Value of Humanities in Executive Development." *Sloan Management Review.* 32: 84–89.

Vaughn, Diane. 1996. *The Challenger Launch Decision.* Chicago: University of Chicago Press.

Velasquez, Manuel. 1988. *Business Ethics.* Second edition. Englewood Cliffs, NJ: Prentice-Hall.

Vidaver-Cohen, Deborah. 1997. "Moral Imagination in Organizational Problem-Solving: An Institutional Perspective." *Business Ethics Quarterly.* 7: 1–26.

Walzer, Michael. 1983. *Spheres of Justice.* New York: Basic Books.

———. 1994. *Thick and Thin.* Notre Dame, IN: Notre Dame University Press.

Weaver, Gary, and Dennis Gioia. 1994. "Paradigms Lost: Incommensurability vs. Structurationist Inquiry." *Organization Studies.* 15: 565–590.

Weick, Karl. 1969; 1979. *The Social Psychology of Organizing.* Reading, MA: Addison-Wesley.

———. 1995. *Sensemaking in Organizations.* Thousand Oaks, CA: Sage Publications.

Werhane, Patricia H., ed. 1984. *Philosophical Issues in Art.* Englewood Cliffs, NJ: Prentice-Hall.

———. 1985. *Persons, Rights, and Corporations.* Englewood Cliffs, NJ: Prentice-Hall.

———. 1988. "Two Ethical Issues in Mergers and Acquisitions." *Journal of Business Ethics.* 7: 41–45.

———. 1990a. "Introducing Morality to Thrift Decision Making." *Stanford Law and Policy Review.* 2: 125–131.

———. 1990b. "Mergers, Acquisitions, and the Market for Corporate Control." *Public Affairs Quarterly.* 4: 81–96.

———. 1991a. *Adam Smith and His Legacy for Modern Capitalism.* New York: Oxford University Press.

———. 1991b. "Engineers and Management: The Challenge of the Challenger Incident." *Journal of Business Ethics.* 10: 605–616.

———. 1992. *Skepticism, Rules, and Private Languages.* Atlantic Highlands, NJ: Humanities Press.

———. 1997. "The Compatibility of Freedom, Equality, and a Communitarian Notion of the Self." In Jonathan Schonscheck and Larry May eds., *Liberty, Equality, and Plurality.* Lawrence: University of Kansas Press.

———. 1998. "Moral Imagination and Management Decision-Making." *Business Ethics Quarterly,* forthcoming.

Westra, Laura, and Patricia H. Werhane. 1998. *The Business of Consumption.* Totowa, NJ: Rowman and Littlefield.

Wicks, Andrew, and R. Edward Freeman. 1990. "A Note on Obedience to Authority." University of Virginia Darden Graduate School Foundation, #E-070. Charlottesville, VA: Darden School, University of Virginia.

Wittgenstein, Ludwig. 1953. *Philosophical Investigations.* Trans. G. E. M. Anscombe. New York: Macmillan.

Woods, Michael. 1983. "Kant's Transcendental Schematism." *Dialectica.* 37: 201–220.

Yates, Brock. 1986. "Audi's Runaway Trouble with the 5000." *Washington Post Magazine.* December 21, W31.

Young, Michael J. 1988. "Kant's View of Imagination." *Kantstudien.* 79: 140–164.

Zimbardo, Philip. 1973. "A Pirandelian Prison." *New York Times Magazine.* April 8, 38–62.

Zipser, Andy. 1989. "Cooking the Books: How Pressure to Raise Sales Led Mini-Scribe to Falisfy Numbers." *Wall Street Journal.* September 11, A1, A8.

Zverina, Jan A. 1989. "Government Says Sudden Acceleration Due to 'Pedal Misapplication.'" *Washington Post.* March 8, F1, F5.

INDEX